ESSENTIAL LAND LAW

SECOND EDITION

Cavendish
Publishing
Limited

London • Sydney

Titles in the series:

ESSENTIAL
LAND LAW

SECOND EDITION

Iris Williams BA, LLB, M Ed, Dip Ed, Barrister

Cavendish
Publishing
Limited

London • Sydney

First published in Great Britain 1994 by Cavendish Publishing Limited, The Glass House, Wharton Street, London WC1X 9PX

Telephone: 0171-278 8000   Facsimile: 0171-278 8080

e-mail: info@cavendishpublishing.com

Visit our Home Page on http://www.cavendishpublishing.com

© Williams, I 1997

First edition 1994

Williams, Iris
Essential Land Law – 2nd ed – (Essential law series)
1. Real property – England 2. Real property – Wales
I Title
346.4'2'043

ISBN 1 85941 364 1

Printed and bound in Great Britain

*To the memory of my mother, to whom I
owed a debt I could never repay,
and my father who died far too young,
but left me with a love of learning.*

Foreword

This book is part of the Cavendish Essential series. The books in the series are designed to provide useful revision aids for the hard-pressed student. They are not, of course, intended to be substitutes for more detailed treatises. Other textbooks in the Cavendish portfolio must supply these gaps.

The Cavendish Essential series is now in its second edition and is a well-established favourite among students.

The team of authors bring a wealth of lecturing and examining experience to the task in hand. Many of us can even recall what it was like to face law examinations!

Professor Nicholas Bourne
General Editor, Essential Series
Swansea
Summer 1997

Acknowledgments

For his unfailing support and patience I thank my husband, Norman. Thanks are due too to past students of the Swansea Law School, whose questions and difficulties provided the basis for the hints on answering questions.

Acknowledgements

Preface

This book was always intended to be an aid to revision and a base for tackling examination questions. Students often complain that even when they feel they have understood an issue in land law, they cannot answer questions on it. For this reason question hints are included where they were felt to be helpful.

This second edition has been updated and amended to take into account changes in the law. Chapter 3 on co-ownership and trusts has been radically changed in accordance with the new provisions of the Trusts of Land Appointment of Trustees Act 1996. Chapter 6 on leases has been similarly greatly altered to include the changes to leasehold covenants afforded by the Landlord and Tenant (Covenants) Act 1995, so that students are made aware of the need to consider separately leasehold covenants made before and after the Act came into force.

Iris Williams
Summer 1997

Contents

1 General principles and the 1925 legislation

You should be familiar with the following areas:

- definition of land
- classification of property
- fixtures and fittings
- estates: the 1925 legislation
- other interests in land
- doctrine of notice
- registration of land charges

The definition of land

Section 205(1)(ix) of the Law of Property Act (LPA) 1925 defines land as including:

> ... land of any tenure and mines and minerals, whether or not held apart from the surface, buildings or parts of buildings (whether the division is horizontal, vertical or made in any other way) and other corporeal hereditaments: also a manor, an advowson, and a rent and other incorporeal hereditaments, and an easement, right, privilege, or benefit in, over or derived from land ...

A *Hereditament* is 'real' property which can be inherited.

A *Corporeal hereditament* is tangible 'real' property, ie the land itself and objects attached to it, eg buildings, trees.

Incorporeal hereditaments are intangible objects, eg tithes, easements, covenants.

Note
The definition of land includes things both above and below the surface of the earth although this has been modified by statute, eg the Civil Aviation Act 1972.

Treasure trove belongs to the Crown, ie silver or gold hidden with the intention of later retrieval but where the owner is unknown, and it has not been hidden, it will pass to the finder.

The classification of property

Realty, ie 'real' property is immovable property, like the land itself, subject only to actions *in rem*. Personalty is movable property not necessarily recoverable because it is subject to actions *in personam* and an award of damages only.

Note
Leasehold property is personalty (for historical reasons) but is recoverable by an action *in rem* and as a result it is called a chattel real.

Be careful
If a question that states that X is the owner of the leasehold property where he lives and he leaves his real property to his wife and his personalty to his children, his wife will get nothing because the leasehold property is personalty.

Fixtures and fittings

A purchaser is entitled to fixtures but not to fittings.

In *Holland v Hodgson* (1872) a two-pronged test was established as a method of distinguishing fixtures from fittings:

- the degree of annexation, ie how firmly the object is attached to the land;
- the purpose of the annexation.

The purpose of annexation may negate the first prong. Compare the situation in the following two cases:

D'Enycourt v Gregory (1866)
In this case, the degree of annexation was reinforced by the purpose of annexation. The statues in a garden were held to be not merely statues but part of the design plan of the whole garden.

Leigh v Taylor (1902)
In this case, however, a tapestry attached to a wall on a wooden frame was held not to be a fixture. Its purpose was not to decorate the wall permanently.

Estates: the 1925 legislation

By s 1(1) of the LPA 1925 the number of legal estates was reduced to *two*:

- an estate in fee simple absolute in possession;
- an estate of a term of years absolute.

This means that any other estate cannot be a legal estate. The term *absolute* means that there are no conditions attached to the estate. It cannot be determined, ie terminated, as long as there is someone to inherit it either by will or on intestacy. If there is no one to inherit it, it goes *bona vacantia* to the Crown, since the Crown owns all land.

Possession is defined in s 205(1)(xix) of the LPA 1925 as including 'receipts of rents and profits or the right to receive the same, if any'. A person holding the fee simple *in possession* means that he or she is immediately entitled to the interest. Occupation is not required for possession. The property can be let; possession is evidenced by receipt of rent.

An estate in fee simple absolute in possession is a freehold estate. An estate of a term of years absolute is a leasehold estate.

Problem

There are some estates which although regarded as 'freehold' do not come within the two legal estates of s 1(1) of the LPA 1925. These are modified fee simple estates, for example, determinable fee simple and conditional fee simple estates.

Determinable fee simple estate

This is a fee simple which will determine automatically should a stipulated event occur *but* it must be possible for such an event *never* to occur. If it is bound to happen at some time there is no determinable fee simple estate.

Look for words like: until, during, while, as long as. If the event does occur the estate will revert to the grantor.

Example

To X in fee simple until he marries.

If X marries, the fee simple will revert to the grantor but X may never marry. If X dies unmarried, the fee simple becomes absolute and forms part of X's estate.

Where the fee simple involves a school, museum, church, library, etc it may come within the Revertor of Sites Act (RSA) 1987. Section 7 defines the sites covered by the Act so that when the determining event occurs there is no automatic reversion to the grantor. The property becomes subject to a trust with the grantor and his successors in title becoming beneficiaries under the statutory trust for sale.

Note
But the Trusts of Land and Appointment of Trustees Act (TLATA) 1996 (see Chapter 3) abolishes trusts for sale of land but makes amendments to the RSA 1987 so that the trustees may sell and hold the money for the beneficiaries as under the former trust for sale (ie the trustees do not have to follow the consultation procedures, etc of this new TLATA 1996).

Example
Land and a building to be used as a library is given on the condition 'in fee simple until it ceases to be a library'. Some 60 years later the library is closed.

The property will now revert to the grantor or his estate under s 7 of the RSA 1987. This is to prevent the trustees claiming it under adverse possession. The trustees hold for the grantor or his estate under a trust.

Conditional fee simple estate
Here the fee simple is subject to a condition which may be:

- a condition precedent: required to be fulfilled before the fee simple can vest in the grantee.

Example
To X in fee simple provided he becomes a barrister. If X never becomes a barrister, it remains with the grantor:

- condition subsequent: where a condition which, if fulfilled, after the fee simple has vested, determines it.

Example
To Z in fee simple provided he never becomes a barrister. If Z subsequently becomes a barrister, the grantor has the right to enter the property and determine the grant.

Look for words such as: provided that, but if, on condition that.

Note
- The difference between a conditional and determinable fee simple is often very difficult to define, as Megarry stated:

> ... the difference is equivalent to that between an eleven inch ruler and a foot ruler with an inch cut off.

- Some conditions are not acceptable as being against public policy, for example, to Mary until she lives with her husband again (determinable fee simple); to Mary on condition she never lives with her husband again (condition precedent).

  These are void.

- Some conditions are void for uncertainty, for example, to Mary until she ceases to reside at Redroofs (determinable fee simple); to Mary provided that she resides at Redroofs (condition precedent).

  'Reside' is uncertain.

Other interests in land

Legal interests

Section 1(2) of the LPA 1925 lists interests in land which are capable of existing as legal interests, ie rights *in rem* (good against all the world). These are:

(a) An easement, right or privilege in or over land equivalent to an estate in fee simple absolute in possession or a term of years absolute.

(b) A rent charge in possession issuing out of charge on land being either perpetual or for a term of years absolute. This means land where annuities, covenants incurring expenditure or other such charges must be met.

Note
Under the Rent Charges Act 1977, no new rent charges can be imposed (except for certain specified ones, for example, under family arrangements) and existing ones must cease within 60 years of 1978.

(c) A charge by way of a legal mortgage.

(d) Any other similar charge on the land which is not created by an instrument.

(e) Rights of entry exercisable over, or in respect of, a legal term of years absolute, or annexed, for any purpose, to a legal rent charge.

Note
Section (e) included land where it was the custom (eg in the Bristol area) to sell land by asking the purchase price and a payment called a rent

charge to be paid at intervals. Default on payment of the rent charge gave a right of re-entry so that the estate could not be a legal one because it was not a fee simple absolute, but subject to the rent charge payment condition. To overcome this the Law of Property (Amendment) Act 1926 amended s 7 of the LPA 1925 by adding 'a fee simple subject to a legal or equitable right of entry or re-entry for the purposes of this Act is a fee simple absolute', so now such an estate comes within s 1(1) of the LPA 1925 as a fee simple absolute in possession.

Equitable interests

The effect of s 1(3) of the LPA 1925 is to make all other interests equitable.

The doctrine of notice

Legal interests are rights *in rem* and, as such, are good against the whole world, whereas equitable rights are not.

Before the 1925 legislation, when land was not registered, equitable interests were subject to the doctrine of notice. This meant that a purchaser was only bound by equitable interests if he was not 'equity's darling', ie not a *bona fide* purchaser for valuable consideration *without* notice of the interests.

Notice may be:

- actual; or
- imputed or implied (ie *via* an agent for example a solicitor); or
- constructive, ie deemed to have been given under the rule in *Hunt v Luck* (1902) that a purchaser must make sufficient and correct enquiries, ie if a purchaser could have discovered the interest if he had made the necessary enquiries he is deemed to have had constructive notice.

In *Kingsnorth Finance Trust Co Ltd v Tizard* (1986), W had an equitable interest in the matrimonial home which was held in her husband's name. H and W quarrelled and W left the house returning to sleep only when H was away, and to get the children to school each day, etc. H took out a loan with a finance company. The finance company sent a surveyor to look at the house; the surveyor knew H was married but believed H when he said that W lived elsewhere because they were separated. The surveyor sent a report to the finance company which stated that although there were children in the house the wife was not an occupant.

It was held that the finance company had *imputed* notice of the *constructive* notice of the surveyor. Had the surveyor looked in the wardrobe and seen W's clothes he would have known she was still in occupation.

The finance company was bound by W's equitable interest.

The Land Charges Act 1972

The Land Charges Act (LCA) 1925 now the LCA 1972 concerns only *unregistered* land and gives protection of equitable interests by registration under one of the Classes A to F. For most purposes Classes C, D and F suffice.

Be careful
The *land charges* register applies to *unregistered* land only, whereas the *charges* register applies to *registered* land.

Class C land charges

(i)   Puisne mortgage, ie a *legal* mortgage not protected by the deposit of title deeds. It is usually a second mortgage and is an exception to the general rule that land charges protect equitable interests.
(ii) A 'limited owner's charge'. This is where a tenant for life places a charge on the land charges register.
(iii) 'A general equitable charge'. This is defined in s 2(4) of the LCA 1972. It includes an equitable mortgage of a legal estate not protected by the deposit of title deeds.
(iv) An estate contract.

Class D land charges

(i)   An Inland Revenue charge when inheritance tax is outstanding.
(ii) Restrictive covenants created after 1 January 1926 and not contained in a lease.
(iii) Equitable easements created after 1 January 1926.

Class F land charges

Class F land charges are charges made under the Matrimonial Homes Act 1983 relating to a spouse's right of occupation of the matrimonial home.

7

Problems

Registration of a land charge

Interests are registered in the name of the owner of the estate which is affected by that interest: however, the problem is that the name of the owner may not be known.

In *Diligent Finance Co Ltd v Alleyne* (1972), a Class F land charge registered under 'Erskine Alleyne' was declared void because her husband's full name was Erskine Owen Alleyne.

Where a lease is purchased it is not always possible to discover the name of the freehold owner. This means that the purchaser may not know of land charges previously registered against the land but by virtue of s 198 of the LPA 1925 he is bound by them (*White v Bijou Mansions Ltd* (1937)).

Class C (iv) problems – estate contracts

Estate contracts include contracts for sale, lease or mortgage, equitable leases, options to purchase and rights of pre-emption. Sometimes more than one of these is registered so that the question of priority arises.

In *Pritchard v Briggs* (1980), both an option to purchase and a right of pre-emption were registered as Class C(iv) land charges on the same property. The right of pre-emption was registered first.

It was held that the option to purchase had priority. The pre-emption was merely a hope (a mere *spes successionis*); it was not an interest in land even though it was registrable.

In *Armstrong and Holmes Ltd v Holmes* (1993), a grant of an option to purchase was registered as a Class C(iv) land charge. When negotiations as to selling price broke down because the vendor refused to take part, the option was taken up in writing. This exercise of taking up the option in writing was not registered as an estate contract under a Class C(iv) land charge. Some of the land was then sold to another party who contended that:

- The exercise of the option had been in writing but not as s 2 of the Law of Property (Miscellaneous Provisions) Act (LP(MP)A) 1989 required because it was not signed by both parties.
- It was also not registered as a Class C(iv) land charge so it was void against him as a purchaser of a legal estate for valuable consideration.

It was held that although the grant of an option must meet the requirements of s 2 of the LP(MP)A 1989 this was not the case on the exercise of an option. The purchaser was bound because the grant of the option was registered as an estate contract (Class C(iv) land charge).

Class D(iii) land charge – equitable easements

A right of re-entry for breach of covenant has been held not to be registrable as an equitable easement.

In *Shiloh Spinners v Harding* (1973), the House of Lords stated that re-entry is subject to the doctrine of notice.

Problems arising from priority of interests

For instance, does creation or registration take priority in unregistered land interests? The equitable maxim 'where the priorities are equal, the first in time prevails' applies to the creation not the registration of interests.

In *McCarthy and Stone Ltd v Julian S Hodge & Co Ltd* (1971), an option to purchase property, ie an estate contract, was not immediately registered. Shortly after, an equitable mortgage was created by the deposit of title deeds; this was registered as a Class D(iii) land charge. Later the option to purchase was registered as a Class C(iv) land charge.

It was held that the estate contract had priority. Although it had been registered last, it had been created first. For the position in regard to mortgages, see Chapter 10.

Interests not registrable as land charges

The following are not registrable as land charges:

- Some interests created before 1 January 1926
  For example, easements and restrictive covenants, created before 1 January 1926.

- Equitable rights of entry
  See *Shiloh Spinners v Harding* (above).

- Interests which can be *overreached*
  That is, beneficial interests under a strict settlement and interests subject under a trust of land (provided certain conditions are satisfied), which are considered in later chapters. Overreaching occurs when property, subject to a trust, is sold and the money is paid to two trustees so that the beneficial interests are in the capital sum (ie the purchase money) and not in land. The doctrine of notice still applies where land is unregistered.

In *Caunce v Caunce* (1969), H and W both contributed to the purchase of the matrimonial home so that W had a beneficial interest under a trust for sale. (Trusts for sale were abolished by the TLATA 1996.) The legal title to the property was in H's name only. H took out mortgages on the house without W's knowledge. He defaulted and the bank claimed possession.

It was held that the bank took the property free of W's beneficial interest which had been *overreached* because the bank had no notice, actual, implied or constructive, of W's interest so they did not know that payment was required to two trustees.

Note

Overreaching strictly is applicable to strict settlements only. At the time of *Caunce v Caunce* trusts for sale came within the doctrine of conversion but the term was applied widely to both. The position has been changed by the TLATA 1996. This is dealt with in more detail in Chapter 3.

The effect of non-registration of a registrable interest as a land charge

Note the effect of ss 4(2), (5) and (8) of the LCA 1972:

- Sections 4(2) and 4(5) mean that where there can be registration of an interest as a land charge and this has not been done, then that interest is void 'as against a purchaser, the land charged with it or of any interest in such land'. This applies to all land charges except Class C(iv) (an estate contract) and Class D.
- Section 4(8) means that in the case of Class C(iv), an estate contract, and of Class D, the interest will be void only as against a purchaser for valuable consideration.

Interests which are protectable by registration as a land charge are void against a purchaser for valuable consideration if they are not registered at the time of purchase (*Hollington Bros Ltd v Rhodes* (1951)).

It does not matter if at the time of purchase the purchaser knew of the interest that had not been registered.

In *Midland Bank Trust Co Ltd v Green* (1981), a father granted his son an option to buy a farm. The son did not register his option as an estate contract, ie a Class C(iv) land charge. Father and son quarrelled and the father then sold the farm to his wife for a nominal sum. The son then indicated his intention to register his interest. Before he did so his mother died, and as a result he claimed the right to exercise his option.

It was held that his option to purchase was void. His mother had provided valuable consideration even though she had only paid a nominal sum. The fact that she knew of his option was irrelevant because he had not registered it.

This means that the requirement of 'good faith' implicit in the doctrine of notice does not apply where an interest in unregistered land can be registered as a land charge and has not been so registered.

The recent case of *Lloyd's Bank v Carrick* (1996) affirms that if an equitable interest in unregistered land is not registered as a land charge, then a purchaser of such land is not bound by that interest even though the owner of the equitable interest is actually occupying that land. This is in sharp contrast to the position in registered land (see Chapter 2).

2 Land registration

You should be familiar with the following areas:

- aims and principles
- registers
- protection of interests
- rectification
- problems
- recommendations of the Law Commissioners

Aims and principles

Registration is largely governed by the Land Registration Act (LRA) 1925 and is compulsory for all legal transfers of land from 1 December 1990.

Aims

The aims of registration are:

- to remove the necessity for title deeds;
- to remove the necessity for searches, making conveyancing easier since all information is on the land certificate.

Principles

The principles of registration are the:

- mirror principle – all facts are 'mirrored' on the register accurately, ie all details about the land are correct;
- curtain principle – some facts are kept secret, for example, interests behind a trust;
- insurance principle – a State guarantee that the information on the register is correct.

The register

This is, in fact, three registers: the property register, the proprietorship register and the charges register.

The property register

The property register, ie a register of the estate, describes the land, eg 11 Whitestone Lane in the District of Clayfield in the County of Essex. It states the type of the estate, whether freehold or leasehold, and the title number assigned to the property. The property register also has a reference to the plan filed on it. A plan of the estate is attached to all property registers of an estate.

The proprietorship register

The proprietorship register gives the name and address of the registered owner, the nature of the estate's title, and any restrictions on the ownership.

Note
There are several categories of title: absolute title is the highest and is given when the registrar deems that title cannot be challenged.

Note
When land is registered a land certificate is issued summarising the entry in the register. This replaces title deeds as evidence of title. Title may be of several types:

- Absolute – the best title.
- Good leasehold.
- Possessory – where the registrar is not absolutely convinced of title, for example, where there is adverse possession or where title deeds have been lost. If the registrar is later satisfied of title this may be upgraded.
- Qualified – where there is some defect with title.

The charges register

The charges register shows all encumbrances on the land.

The protection of interests

Minor interests

There are four methods of entry on the charges register:

- *Notice:* registrable only if the land certificate is produced; this includes estate contracts, certain charges, options to purchase, restrictive covenants, equitable easements, right of occupation by a spouse.
- *Restriction*: this prevents dealings unless a condition is fulfilled; it is used for settled land or land held under a trust for sale.
- *Caution*: used where the cautioner wishes to be warned of any dealings concerning the land but where he cannot obtain the land certificate.

Note

Chancery plc v Ketteringham (1994) – a caution is simply designed to warn of any proposed dealing.

- *Inhibition:* used in bankruptcy or in any emergency.

Note

A purchaser will not be bound by any minor interest unless it is entered on the register even if he knew of it *before* the purchase (s 59(6) of the LRA 1925).

Overriding interests

These are *not* registrable. Any purchaser is bound by them whether or not he knew of their existence. Overriding interests are an exception to the mirror principle.

Rectification of the register

Section 82 of the LRA 1925

Rectification of the register is only possible on certain specified grounds. These are:

- to give effect to an overriding interest (*Chowood Ltd v Lyall (No 2)* (1930); see Chapter 9 on Adverse Possession);
- where there is fraud or lack of care on the part of the registered proprietor causing the error;
- where it is equitable to do so.

In *Norwich and Peterborough Building Society v Steed* (1992), D went abroad and gave his mother power to deal with his house. By means of fraud his sister and her husband persuaded the mother to convey the house to them. They later mortgaged it and then defaulted on the loan. The mortgagee sought possession. On returning D sought rectification of the register so that he was again shown as proprietor and he also wanted the removal of the mortgagee's charge on the house. It was held that:

- Since his mother had consented to the sale it was not void, but because it had resulted from a fraud it was voidable; the mortgagees had obtained a good title since they had acted in good faith.
- There would be rectification of the register so that the names of his sister and her husband would be removed and his name substituted.
- Section 82(1) of the LRA 1925 gave the court a discretion to rectify where it was equitable to do so. It was equitable as regards D's name, but there would be no rectification to remove the building society's charge because it was not void and the society had not been involved in the fraud.

Section 83 of the LRA 1925 allows an indemnity to be paid for loss suffered if there is an error or an omission on the register. However, s 83 does not allow for rectification to give effect to an overriding interest because, then, there is deemed to be no such loss (see Chapter 9 on Adverse Possession).

Note
Section 2 of the LRA 1997 means that where a person has suffered loss because of error or an omission on the register, he or she may be indemnified, and this is even if there is no actual rectification of the register.

Problems

The relationship between s 20(1) and s 59(6) of the LRA 1925

Section 20(1) of the LRA 1925
Section 20(1) ensures that minor interests which are registered are protected; if they are not protected they are void.

Section 59(6) of the LRA 1925
Section 59(6) ensures that a purchaser takes free of any unregistered interest whether or not he had notice of it and whether that notice was actual, implied or constructive.

In *Peffer v Rigg* (1977), the marriage broke up. H held the legal title of the matrimonial home but his brother-in-law had contributed towards the purchase price. H sold the house to W for the nominal sum of £1.00. W *knew* H held the house on a trust for sale for his brother-in-law whose interest had not been registered.

It was held that s 59(6) applied to a purchaser in good faith because this is how a purchaser is defined in s 3(xxi) of the LRA 1925. W was not such a purchaser because she knew of the trust for sale, therefore, reading s 20(1) and s 59(6) together she held on a constructive trust for the brother-in-law.

The doctrine of notice was held to prevail despite the fact that the land was registered.

Comment

This interpretation of *Peffer v Rigg* has been subject to criticism (Dixon, M, *Lecture Notes on Land Law*, 1994, London: Cavendish Publishing). Dixon contends that the dicta in the case 'suggests it is always "fraud" or "bad faith" to ignore an unprotected minor interest of which you are aware and should not be regarded as good law'; the decision is really one relying on the maxim that 'equity will not permit a statute to be used as an instrument of fraud'.

Lyus v Prowsa Developments Ltd (1982) is another case illustrating that s 20(1) does not always prevail.

The diagram below illustrates the essential facts of *Lyus v Prowsa Developments Ltd* (1982).

Bank mortgagees who have lent to

$\downarrow$

Developers of estate who   Contract to sell to Lyus
go bankrupt. $\longrightarrow$ but transfer to be
Bank takes over.   completed only when
     house built.

$\downarrow$

Bank sells to Prowsa
Developments Ltd subject
to contract with Lyus.

$\downarrow$

Sells to a third party: no reference to Lyus contract in conveyance.

The registered land was developed as a housing estate. There was a contract to sell but there was to be no completion until a house was built; before this happens the mortgagees sell because the developers go bankrupt. The mortgagees, ie the bank, include a clause that the sale is subject to the contract with Lyus. The property is bought by Prowsa who sell to a third party without reference to the contract.

All the sales were registered except the agreement between the Bank and Prowsa regarding the Lyus contract.

The court decided that Prowsa held on a constructive trust for Lyus; otherwise it would be fraud. This constructive trust was also imposed on the third party because they could not be free of the contract. In this instance, a minor interest, unprotected on the register, was enforced.

Competing minor interests

Section 20 of the LRA 1925 protects all registered minor interests but where competing interests are registered, the equitable principle 'the first in time prevails', ie such interests are ranked by date of creation not the date of entry on the register.

This means that where a minor interest has been registered it will *not* take priority over a minor interest that has not been registered but was *created* earlier.

Barclays Bank v Taylor (1974) (which established that the position regarding priority is the same for registered and unregistered land) was followed in *Mortgage Corporation v Nationwide Credit Corporation* (1993) despite the fact that the Law Commission 1987 wanted this position reversed, and the date of registration to determine priority.

Overriding interests: s 70(1) of the LRA 1925

Overriding interests are not registrable but bind any purchaser so that they are an exception to the mirror principle of registration. This means that the purchaser is put on enquiry as if the land were unregistered.

Problems inherent in overriding interests themselves

Section 70(1)(a)
Section 70(1)(a) includes easements and profits. It is unclear whether it covers equitable as well as legal easements and profits. In *Celsteel Ltd v Alton House Holdings Ltd* (1985), it was held that equitable easements can be overriding but there is still a problem because of the interpretation of 'not required to be protected' in s 70(1)(a).

Section 70(1)(g)

> ... the rights of every person in actual occupation of the land or in receipt of the rents and profits thereof, save where enquiry is made of such person and the rights are not disclosed.

This means that:

- the right must be in the land itself; and
- the person who has the right is in actual occupation of the land; or in receipt of its rents and profits; and
- the purchaser must have enquired 'of such person' and not been told of the right. This means effectively that the rule in *Hunt v Luck* (1902) used in unregistered land applies, though the doctrine of notice does *not* apply to registered land.

Be careful

Occupation is not enough for s 70(1)(g) to apply; the occupier must also have a right in the land.

In *Strand Securities v Caswell* (1965) Mr Caswell allowed his stepdaughter to occupy his flat, rent free. He held the flat on a sub-lease. When the landlord sold the flat the purchasers sought to take it free of Mr Caswell's sub-lease.

It was held that the purchasers were allowed to take the flat free of Mr Caswell's sub-lease. Although Mr Caswell had a right in the land, s 70(1)(g) did not apply since he was not in actual occupation. Compare this with *Williams and Glyn's Bank v Boland* (1981) in which H and W purchased a matrimonial home both contributing to the purchase price. The house was registered in H's name only. H mortgaged the house to the bank; W was unaware of this. H defaulted on the mortgage payments and the bank sought possession.

The court held that W had a beneficial interest by virtue of her contribution to the purchase price. She was also in actual occupation and she therefore had an overriding interest under s 70(1)(g) of the LRA 1925 and the bank was bound by it.

Note

Mrs Boland's interest was under a trust for sale (see Chapter 3 on Trust for Sale). Had her interest been overreached by payment to two trustees the bank would have taken free of it. (See *City of London Building Society v Flegg* (1988), also in Chapter 3, where it was held that when payment is made to two trustees an overriding interest is overreached.)

Note

Trusts for sale no longer exist – see Chapter 3.

In *Skipton Building Society v Clayton* (1993), it was held that if a person is in actual occupation then they have an overriding interest under s 70(1)(g) even if his or her occupation is not discoverable.

Section 70(1)(k)

Leases not exceeding 21 years are classified as overriding interests.

The Law Commission's recommendations 1987

The Law Commission recommended that:

- Overriding interests be restricted to:
  - (a) legal easements and profits only so that *Celsteel Ltd v Alton House Holdings* (1985) would not apply to include equitable easements;
  - (b) rights acquired by adverse possession;
  - (c) leases of 21 years;
  - (d) customary rights.
- All overriding interests under s 70 be abolished except for s 70(1)(g), rights by actual occupation.
- Any other interests to be minor interests only.
- Rectification indemnity provisions be extended to include loss resulting from an overriding interest, ie *Re Chowood's Registered Land* (1933) would be reversed.
- Restriction and inhibition to have a very restricted use.
- Any unprotected minor interest should be void against a purchaser for valuable consideration who acted in good faith.
- A protected minor interest always has priority over an earlier but unprotected one, ie reversing *Barclays Bank v Taylor* (1974). That this has not been accepted is illustrated by *Mortgage Corporation v Nationwide Credit Corporation* (1993) which recently affirmed the case of *Barclays Bank v Taylor*.

The recommendations have not been implemented.

3 Co-ownership and trusts of land

You should be familiar with the following areas:

Co-ownership creation

- severance

Trusts and the effect of the TLATA 1996

- trustees
- beneficiaries
- resulting and constructive trusts
- occupation and beneficial interest
- spouses and occupation
- implied consents

Co-ownership

Co-ownership arises when two or more persons hold an estate at the same time, ie concurrently, when this occurs:

- The legal estate must be held by all of them as joint tenants or by one or a number of them on trust for themselves and for the others. Before the Trusts of Land and Appointment of Trustees Act (TLATA) 1996 came into being on 1 January 1997, such trusts were trusts for sale; they are now trusts of land.
  Section 36 of the Law of Property Act (LPA) 1925 states that a legal estate can only be held as joint tenants. There can only be four joint tenants of a legal estate, ie the first four named.
- The equitable interests may be held as joint tenants or as tenants in common.

Where the equitable interests are held as joint tenants

Joint tenants are entitled to the whole of the estate. As joint tenants, they cannot identify any part of it as theirs individually. This means that if one dies, the surviving joint tenants still hold the whole of the estate. This is the *right of survivorship* or the *jus accrescendi*, so that even if the deceased joint owner left a will in which he bequeathed his estate to his friend X, X who is not a joint tenant, would receive nothing.

Where the equitable interests are held as tenants in common

When individuals can claim an identified share in the land, they hold the equitable interests as tenants in common. Each has an undivided share in the land. This means that the whole estate can be identified in terms of divided shares so each can identify his share.

Look for words 'in equal shares', 'equally', etc. When a tenant in common dies, his share will go as directed by his will or to his next of kin on intestacy.

Example

> *Legal estate held by husband and wife as joint tenants*
> *(required by s 36 of the LPA 1925)*
> *They have four children A, B, C, D*

Husband and wife are joint tenants in equity	Husband and wife are tenants in common in equity
H by will leaves his interest to A, B, C, D	H by will leaves his interest to A, B, C, D

Husband dies

His wife receives whole estate	His wife receives her half share
H's will is void and A, B, C, D receive nothing	A, B, C, D receive the remaining half – one-eighth each

The creation of a joint tenancy

The creation of a joint tenancy requires:
- The four unities. These are:

(a) unity of possession (ie the whole property must be held jointly);

(b) unity of interest (where every joint tenant must have an interest of the same nature and extent, ie all the tenants must hold the same freehold estate or leasehold estate);

(c) unity of time (where all the interests must vest at the same time);

(d) unity of title (where the title must be obtained in the same way, eg under the same conveyance).

- There must be no words of severance, for example, in equal shares, to A and B equally.
- There must be no rule of equity against the joint tenancy.

Note

'Equity leans against joint tenancies' and there is an equitable presumption against a joint tenancy:

- where there is a partnership (for commercial reasons). This presumption can be negated by an express clause against it;
- where two or more persons advance money on a mortgage even if the advance is of different amounts;
- where persons purchasing property contribute different amounts, and hold the legal title as joint tenants, equity presumes they hold the equitable interests as tenants in common;
- where there is ownership of land for multiple business purposes. This was a category the Privy Council established in *Malayan Credit Ltd v Jack Chia Mph Ltd* (1986), although Privy Council decisions are persuasive only.

Remember

The legal estate can only ever be held as joint tenants (s 36 of the LPA 1925) even if the equitable joint tenancy is severed.

Severance of an equitable joint tenancy

Severance can be by:

- *Written notice (s 36(2) of the LPA 1925)*
  This does not require written consent from the other joint tenants. It is sufficient under s 196 of the LPA 1925 that the notice is sent to the address of any other joint tenant (by recorded delivery) even if it is not received by the person to whom it is sent (*Re 88 Berkeley Road, London NW9* (1971)).

- *Such other acts or things*
  '... as would have been effectual to sever the tenancy' (s 36(2) of the LPA 1925). There are conflicting cases as to what constitutes such acts. In *Re Draper's Conveyance* (1969) the husband and wife were joint tenants both as to the legal and equitable interests of a house. W obtained a decree *nisi* but a decree absolute had not yet been granted. W issued a summons supported by an affidavit for the sale of the house and division of proceeds. H remained in the house but died intestate before it was sold. The court held that the summons and affidavit constituted sufficient notice of severance and, therefore, his estate went to H's next of kin.

  In *Harris v Goddard* (1983), the husband remarried and lived in the house inherited from his first wife. His second wife petitioned for a divorce and asked for an order under s 24 of the Matrimonial Causes Act 1973 that is a transfer and/or settlement of the former home. H then died. It was held that the petition did not constitute sufficient notice of severance. W inherited the house and H's children from his first marriage got nothing. W inherited under *jus accrescendi*. She had not severed the joint tenancy.

  The difference between these two cases is that the intention must be to sever *immediately*, not at some time in the future, ie a desire to end is insufficient, something must be done to make that desire an immediate intention.

  In a recent case, *Hunter v Babbage* (1994), H and W were both legal and beneficial joint tenants. The marriage broke down and they were divorced. W then applied for ancillary relief. After discussions a draft agreement was arranged for the sale of the property so that the proceeds could be divided (ie there was to be severance). Before an actual agreement was completed H died.

  It was held that the equitable joint tenancy had been severed by the draft agreement so that a half share of the beneficial interest went to H's estate. A joint tenant could determine his or her tenancy when- ever he or she wished, even where there was no express agreement to sever but where such an intention could be inferred. In this case, a common intention to sever could be inferred (*cf Burgess v Rawnsley* (1975)).

- *Mutual agreement*
  This is where there has been a decision to sever by both parties.
  In *Burgess v Rawnsley* (1975), Mrs Rawnsley met a widower at a reli- gious rally. Some time later they agreed to buy the house in which

he was a tenant. Each paid half of the purchase price and became both joint legal and equitable owners. Mrs Rawnsley refused to marry the widower and so he decided to buy her out and offered her £750 for her interest. She orally agreed but later changed her mind and asked for £1,000, which he refused. When the widower died the question of severance arose. The court held that the oral agreement was a sufficient act of severance, there was a clear intention evinced by both parties that they should hold the equitable interest as tenants in common so Mrs Rawnsley was only entitled to a half-share.

- *Alienation*
  Severance by alienation can be by sale to a stranger or by a joint tenant mortgaging his equitable interest.
- *Bankruptcy*
  This is a particular form of alienation. In *Re Palmer (decd)* (1993), a man died virtually bankrupt though no bankruptcy order had been filed against him. An insolvency administration order was obtained against his estate. The trustee appointed under the order sought a declaration that he was trustee at the time of the death. If he obtained such a declaration, then there would have been severance of the joint tenancy of property in which his wife was the other joint tenant. The wife appealed against the initial decision and the Appeal Court upheld the wife's claim that the administration order took effect when the person died, not on the first moment of the day he died. This meant there had been no severance and the wife was entitled to the entire property.

Remember

If a joint tenancy as to the equitable interest is severed, the legal estate is *still* held on a joint tenancy.

Example

A, B and C hold as joint tenants as to the legal and equitable interests. A severs his equitable interest.

A, B and C continue to hold the legal estate as joint tenants. B and C still hold their equitable interests as joint tenants but A holds his equitable interest as a tenant in common.

If A dies, the legal estate is held by B and C as joint tenants. B and C hold their equitable interest as joint tenants but A's share passes to his heir by will or on intestacy.

Rent and the rights of co-owners as landlords

The traditional common law view is that where there is a joint tenancy, and one joint owner leaves, he cannot force the other (or others) to pay rent when he (or they) remain in the property.

But

In *Dennis v McDonald* (1982), where the cohabitees held the legal title as joint tenants and the equitable interests as tenants in common, it was held that the ousted cohabitee was entitled to compensation from the person who remained in the house and this was assessed as half a fair rent.

In *Re Pavlou (a bankrupt)* (1993), where H and W were legal and equitable joint tenants, it was held that despite the common law rule that one co-owner cannot be forced to pay rent to another, if one remains in the home, equity will intervene, if it is necessary to ensure justice between the parties and will order the co-owner in occupation to pay rent.

It does not matter if the spouse who left the home did so voluntarily.

Illegality

Even if co-ownership is established in order to defraud, an equitable interest claimed under it will not be void unless the illegal act, itself, is relied upon to establish the interest.

In *Tinsley v Milligan* (1993), two women purchased a house together but the legal title was conveyed into the name of only one of them with the intention that both should have an equitable interest in the property. This was done to defraud the DSS (ie so that the other could claim benefit illegally).

The court found that there was a resulting trust (see p 32) and a beneficial interest under it for the one who did not hold the legal title. She *had* contributed to the purchase price.

Co-ownership, equity and trusts of land

Co-ownership involves concurrent interests and where there are concurrent interests in property, until the TLATA 1996 (in force 1 January 1997), the estate was held under a trust for sale (s 36 of the LPA 1925). Nearly all such trusts for sale have now become trusts of land; the exception is express trusts for sale.

How such a trust for sale arose and the effect of the TLATA 1996

A trust for sale was created:

- by the express words, 'shall hold on trust for sale'. This means that successive interests were created under a trust for sale, ie a settlement but not a strict settlement (see Chapter 4). A limited number of these will remain trusts for sale depending on their wording;
- by statute (s 19(2) of the LPA 1925) where land was conveyed to a minor jointly with one or more persons of full age; and also where land was held by joint tenants (ie co-ownership by virtue of s 36 of the LPA 1925);
- where there was an intestacy the personal representatives held the land on trust for sale under s 33 of the Administration of Estates Act 1925;
- by the court where it was equitable to do so.

Such a trust for sale was 'an immediate, binding trust for sale whether or not exercisable at the request or with the consent of any person, and with or without a power at discretion to postpone sale' (s 205(xxix) of the LPA 1925).

Immediate meant the trust was operative from the moment it was created. If it only became operative in the future it was not a trust for sale but settled land under a strict settlement. (See Chapter 4.)

But since 'equity regards as done that which ought to be done', equity regarded the land as sold immediately the trust was created (whether or not it was actually sold), so that the *doctrine of conversion* came into operation. Under this doctrine, there was a *notional* sale of land so that it was converted into personalty (money) immediately, so that the interests of beneficiaries immediately the trust was created was in money and not in land.

Binding meant there was a duty to sell and this duty was to be fulfilled even if it was postponed indefinitely. Section 25(4) of the LPA 1925 gave the trustees power to postpone (unless the trust was an express trust with a specific clause as to a contrary intention). The duty to sell was under s 35 of the LPA 1925.

All such trusts for sale have now become *trusts of land* and although there is some uncertainty as to how the new TLATA 1996 will actually work, *all* pre-existing trusts for *sale of land* will become *trusts of land*. This means that trustees will no longer have a duty to sell the land. The doctrine of conversion is abolished so that interests remain in land not in money.

The role of the trustees in the new trusts of land under the TLATA 1996

- In effect the trustees become the absolute owners of the land in the sense that they can do what an absolute owner could do, but they may, under ss 6–9 of the TLATA 1996, delegate such powers to an equitable owner of the land.
- The land may still be sold and the purchaser must still obtain a receipt for his purchase money from the trustees. Only these can give a valid receipt. This means the protection existing before the new TLATA 1996 under s 27 of the LPA 1925 continues. The interests of equitable owners may, therefore, still be overreached by the actions of the trustees.
- On the other hand, under s 11 of the new TLATA 1996, trustees must consult the equitable owners as regards the estate and as far as the terms of the trust allow carry out their wishes.
- Unless the terms of the trust state that the trustees can only act in accordance with the wishes of the equitable owners, the trustees have absolute powers over the land (ss 8 and 10 TLATA 1996).

Before the TLATA 1996, if there was a disagreement among trustees as to a sale, *Re Mayo* (1943) was authority that there should be a sale, but then trustees were always under a duty to sell even if it was postponed. There is no such duty under the new TLATA 1996 so *Re Mayo* may not apply.

- The court can impose a term that the trustees' powers are subject to the consent of the equitable owners. Anyone with an interest in the land may apply to the court under s 14 for such an order.
- Section 14 also allows other applications by persons with an interest in the land, eg for an order for sale or to stop the trustees from selling. The conditions under which a court may grant such applications are given in s 15.
- Section 15(1). The matters to which the court must have regard in determining an application for an order under s 14 include:
    (a) the intentions of the person or persons who created the trust;
    (b) the purposes for which the property held subject to trust is held;
    (c) the welfare of any minor who occupies or might reasonably be expected to occupy any land subject to the trust as his home; and
    (d) the interests of any secured creditor of any beneficiary.

Section 15 specifically excludes applications by a trustee of a bankrupt which come within s 335A of the Insolvency Act (IA) 1986.

- Case law under s 30 of the LPA 1925 will still be relevant but not determinant. Under s 30, the beneficiaries of a trust for sale as 'persons interested' could apply to the court for an order to sell if the trustees refused to do so. This would now take place under s 14 of the TLATA 1996 for trusts of land. Under s 30 of the LPA 1925 the court in exercising its discretion would consider all the circumstances including:

  (a) Whether the purpose for which the property was acquired still subsisted.

  In *Jones v Challenger* (1960), property had been bought for the purpose of a matrimonial home. The wife later left. The court held that the purpose for which the property had been bought no longer subsisted and ordered it to be sold.

  In *Bedson v Bedson* (1965), a draper's shop with attached living accommodation was purchased as a business and a matrimonial home. When the marriage ended it was held that the purpose for which the property had been bought still subsisted; it had been to provide the husband with a livelihood and this purpose still subsisted.

  (b) The interests of any children.

  In *Re Evers Trust* (1980), a house was bought by cohabitees. The woman had provided most of the purchase money but the legal title was held in joint names so that each held under a trust for sale for the other. When the couple separated the man applied for an order for sale under s 30 of the LPA 1925. It was held that the order would not be granted because the purpose for which the property had been bought still subsisted; the child of the union still needed a home. Since the man was living with his mother he did not need accommodation. The sale could be postponed until the child left home.

  (c) The interests of creditors in a bankruptcy case. This now comes under s 336 of the IA 1986, which lists the order for the court's consideration as:
    - the interests of the creditors;
    - the conduct of the spouse or ex-spouse as far as it contributed to the bankruptcy;
    - the financial needs and resources of the spouse or ex-spouse;
    - the needs of any children;
    - any other circumstances.

In *Re Citro* (1990), the husband and wife held the beneficial interest of the matrimonial home in equal shares. The trustee in bankruptcy applied for an order for sale so that the husband's share could be used to pay his creditors. There were children of the marriage, the youngest of whom was aged 10; there was no other family home.

The Court of Appeal held that the rights of the creditors took precedence over that of the spouse (and children) whether or not the property was a matrimonial or family home. Although the IA 1986 did not apply in the case, the Court of Appeal stated that s 336 of that Act was meant to apply the same test to exceptional circumstances.

In *Barclays Bank v Hendricks* (1995), a wife with young children was prevented from selling the matrimonial home by her husband's creditor. She could not obtain a deferment of the sale until the children were 18 or ceased full-time education. Quoting *Re Citro*, it was stated that when the spouses were separated the purpose of the property as a matrimonial home no longer existed. There were no exceptional circumstances, the wife could move into another available house.

- Trustees have new powers to buy land for investment, occupation or some other purpose under s 6 of the new TLATA 1996.

Trusts of land; co-ownership, spouses and cohabitees

Before the TLATA 1996, whenever land was conveyed into the names of two or more persons there was a statutory trust for sale so that each held on a trust for sale for the other. This was the effect of s 36 of the LPA 1925.

The TLATA 1996 abolishes statutory trusts for sale. Under s 5 these now become implied trusts of land which impose no duty to sell.

Nevertheless, the same problem arises when the legal title of the land is in the name of one person when another or others have made a contribution to the purchase price. This is a common situation where a matrimonial home is involved or when a property has been purchased by cohabitees. It creates difficulties because:

- s 52 of the LPA 1925 requires that any conveyance of land must be by deed;
- s 53(1)(a) of the LPA 1925 (as amended by the Law of Property (Miscellaneous Provisions) Act 1989) requires all interests in land to be in writing;
- s 53(1)(b) of the LPA 1925 requires a declaration of a trust in land to be 'manifested and proved in writing'.

Married couples and cohabitees often merely make informal agreements between themselves when they purchase property so that only one person satisfies these requirements.

Where it is equitable to do so, the courts have sought to find an equitable interest for the other contributor who cannot satisfy the requirements of the LPA 1925. They have done so by finding a resulting, implied or constructive trust so falling within s 53(2) of the LPA 1925. This states that s 53(1) does not affect the creation or operation of a resulting, implied or constructive trust (which can give rise to a trust of land).

The landmark case of *Neville v Wilson* (1995) considered the relationship between s 53(1)(c) and s 53(2) and affirmed that a constructive trust within s 53(2) of the LPA 1925 dispenses with the requirement of writing under s 53(1)(c).

A resulting trust

A resulting trust arises strictly where property is purchased by two or more persons but the legal title is held by only one or some of them. The court finds the person holding the legal title holds the property on a resulting trust for himself and the other(s) in equity. The equitable interests are in proportion to the contributions to the purchase price, so there must be a direct monetary contribution either as an initial sum or by mortgage instalments or by both.

In *Bull v Bull* (1955), a mother and son purchased a house together but the legal title was in the son's name only. It was held that the son held on a resulting trust for his mother.

Note

In *Halifax Building Society v Brown* (1995), the Appeal Court held that when a married couple are given a loan from one set of parents to purchase a house, the house is implied to be jointly owned even when only one name is on the title, so that the other is deemed to have made a contribution.

Note

The word *purchased*. There will be no resulting trust where there was a *gift* enabling the purchase to take place. A gift confers *no* beneficial interest on the donor. It becomes the property of the donee alone. If he or she uses it to purchase property, he or she alone, will have an interest in that property. The donor will have no interest whatsoever.

A constructive trust

Where there is an agreement between the parties that each should have a beneficial interest in the property, even though only one holds the legal title (ie a common intention as to the beneficial interest) *and* on the basis of such common intention, the person not holding the legal title has made some contribution to the acquisition of the property, albeit an indirect one (ie not by initial payment or mortgage installment), then the courts have found a beneficial interest under a constructive trust.

Note

The distinction between a *resulting trust* as requiring a *direct* contribution and a *constructive trust* as being satisfied by an *indirect* contribution has been blurred by case law and the terms have been used interchangeably. In both cases, the person with the legal title holds it on a trust for sale for himself and the other beneficiaries.

Drake v Whipp (1995) illustrates that lawyers are often no longer clear as to the distinction. There was an appeal on the grounds that the trial judge had confused the 'doctrines of resulting trusts and constructive trusts'. At the Appeal Court, it was held that all that is required for a constructive trust is that there should be a common intention that the party who is not the legal owner should have a beneficial interest and should act to his or her detriment on a reliance on that interest.

Note

If there is an *express declaration* as to who shall have a beneficial interest, then that is conclusive as to where such interests lie regardless of any contributions made to the purchase price, direct or indirect.

In *Goodman v Gallant* (1986), the husband and wife bought a house together. The legal title was in the husband's name but the beneficial interest was declared to be held as joint tenants.

The court held that on severance of the joint tenancy, each spouse held one-half of the proceeds of sale and where there was a declaration of a beneficial joint tenancy it did not matter if their contribution to the purchase price were not equal.

Problems have arisen as to the meaning of common intention and contribution.

Common intention

In *Lloyd's Bank plc v Rosset* (1990), the House of Lords reviewed the cases and set out the conditions where a spouse or cohabitee, not holding legal title, might acquire a beneficial interest in the matrimonial home or property in which they which lived together or had lived together.

For common intention, Lord Bridge found two situations:

• Where there was evidence of *express* discussion that there had been 'any agreement, arrangement or understanding between them' that the property was to be shared beneficially *and* that that express discussion had taken place 'prior' to acquisition or 'exceptionally at some' later date, a common intention might be found. This means that both parties understood there was a common intention and had *expressly* conveyed this understanding to each other.

   If such evidence was forthcoming, then the party claiming a beneficial interest had to show he or she had acted to his or her detriment in reliance on that agreement for there to be a *constructive trust* or proprietary estoppel.

• Where there is no such evidence, Lord Bridge stated the conduct of the parties is the only basis on which an inference of *common intention* that there should be a beneficial interest could arise, and that conduct itself could give rise to a *constructive trust*. He then went on to point out that he doubted whether, in this situation, any conduct other than a direct contribution to the purchase price by initial payment or mortgage instalments would be sufficient.

Express common intention
In previous cases, express common intention has often been inferred.

In *Eves v Eves* (1975), common intention was inferred because, at the time the property was purchased, the defendant put the legal title in his name only, telling the plaintiff that this was because she was under 21 and could not hold the legal title, otherwise he would have put the house in her name. It was held that the lie inferred an *express common intention*.

In *Grant v Edwards* (1986), the legal title was in M's name only. M said this was because otherwise W's divorce proceedings would be jeopardised. Again it was held that the lie inferred an *express common intention*.

In *Burns v Burns* (1984), the couple had been cohabitees for 19 years and had children together. The legal title of the house was in M's name only. M had purchased it.

The court held that no *express common intention* could be inferred. What W had spent, eg on housekeeping, furniture, and clothing for M and the children (she worked when the children were older) was not a contribution to the 'acquisition of the house'. This seems to indicate a shift in thinking back to the position in *Pettit v Pettit* (1970) and *Gissing and Gissing* (1970).

In *Burns v Burns*, Fox LJ said that any claim to a beneficial interest:

> ... must depend on showing a *common intention* that there should
> be such an interest and whether the trust which would arise in
> such circumstances is described as implied, constructive or result-
> ing does not greatly matter ... what is needed is evidence and fur-
> ther that such evidence, can be inferred to be referable to the
> acquisition of the house.

In other words, 'money' is the criterion.

The position as regards common intention expressed in *Lloyd's Bank
v Rosset* was affirmed in *Ivan v Blake* (1993) where it was held that a
direct contribution to the purchase price is required to establish a beneficial interest. When there is no evidence of an express intention that
there should be such interest.

Contribution

Contribution is the second limb of finding a beneficial interest under a
constructive trust (ie where the contribution is not a direct one to the
purchase price or payment of the mortgage instalments), but which
allows the inference of common intention by conduct.

In the earlier cases of *Pettit v Pettit* (1970) and *Gissing v Gissing*
(1970), the House of Lords stated that where a *common intention* was
established that there should be a beneficial interest, and that there
was agreement as to what that contribution should be (otherwise it is
a mere promise and equity will not assist a volunteer), then it must be
an indirect contribution in money or money's worth (this means it
must be strictly referable to payment of the purchase price; contribution in such a way so that without it the spouse or partner holding the
legal title could not pay the mortgage instalments).

An insubstantial contribution (ie not in money or money's worth)
would not suffice. In *Pettit v Pettit*, decorating, gardening, looking
after the children was insufficient.

In the case of *Gissing v Gissing*, being married for 25 years, having a
baby and contributing to the household expenses when this was not
strictly necessary did not suffice.

Increasingly, after 1970 the position was modified. In *Grant v
Edwards* (1986), contributing to household expenses enabling M to
meet the mortgage instalments was a sufficient act of detriment to give
rise to a constructive trust when *common intention* had been inferred.

In *Cooke v Head* (1972), working the cement mixture for a bungalow
the couple intended to live in was sufficient to establish both a *common
intention* and sufficient contribution.

In *Lloyd's Bank v Rosset* (1991), Lord Bridge doubted whether in a situation where there is no evidence of *common intention* whether anything but a direct contribution would suffice to furnish the necessary intention and resultant action in the belief such intention was established. This follows *Burns v Burns* (1984) where the contribution, it was held, must relate directly to the acquisition of the house or its improvement.

In the case of *Hammond v Mitchell* (1991) Waite J said:

> The court first has to ask itself whether there have been, at any time prior to acquisition of the disputed property, or exceptionally at some later date, discussions between the parties leading to agreement, arrangement or understanding reached between them that the property is to be shared beneficially.

He went on to say that if the answer is 'yes', then the court will examine the evidence for conduct, on behalf of the claimant to the beneficial interest, which can be attributed to his or her acts in reliance on that common intention.

If no such common intention was found (ie the answer is no), then the court could still find a *presumed* intention in the actions of the parties.

Quantification of a beneficial interest in co-ownership cases

In *Midland Bank v Cooke* (1995), the matrimonial home was purchased by H's savings, a mortgage and a gift from H's parents. It was in H's name only. Later a larger mortgage was taken out, again in H's name but with the agreement of his wife, who apparently agreed to this second mortgage taking priority over any interest she may have had in the property. When the bank sought possession because of default, the wife claimed she had only agreed to this second mortgage because of undue influence by her husband.

Her sole contribution to the property had been some improvement. The trial judge, however, ruled that the only ground on which she could claim an interest in the property was that the wedding gift was half hers and this gave her an interest worth 6% of the value of the property. The wife appealed.

The Court of Appeal held:
- Once an interest has been established, the court could decide what proportion of the property it represented by examining the dealings in the case and not only the contribution made.

- There had been no discussion as to the actual ownership of the house but it was clear there had been an intention to own it jointly, so the wife had a 50% share.

This case raises problems:
- Contribution to the purchase price gives rise to a resultant trust in proportion to the amount contributed. H made such contribution but W's was only *via* the wedding gift.
- Intention seems to have been presumed, is this in accord with *Rosset*?
- If the basis of an interest is to be improvements to the property, why did the wife not use s 37 of the Matrimonial Proceedings and Property Act (MPPA) 1970 (see p 39).
- What is the evidence for undue influence? (see Chapter 10, Mortgages).

These problems should be discussed because there may be an appeal to the House of Lords and *Rosset* was not cited in the case.

Drake v Whipp (1995) concerned cohabitees who had purchased a barn for conversion. W had provided approximately 40% of the purchase price and 10% of the conversion expenditure. The judge considered her contribution to the purchase price and to the conversion to be only a contribution to the purchase price expressed as a percentage of it. This means he considered her contribution to give rise to a resulting trust only. She appealed.

The Appeal Court held that there was, in fact, a constructive trust. There had been a common intention and she had acted to her detriment by contributing to the conversion costs in reliance on that intention.

As a result her interest was one-third of the value of the property.

In Huntingford v Hobbs (1993), two people bought property agreeing that one of them, W, would supply the difference between the purchase price and the sum they received on a mortgage. The other, M, would pay the mortgage instalments. The legal title was held in both names but they had never discussed the beneficial interests.

It was held that each had an interest quantified with reference to the actual sums each had paid at the time of the initial purchase. Their common intention at the time had been that W should have a beneficial interest in proportion to the difference between the purchase price and the sum obtained on mortgage, and M, who had agreed to pay the mortgage instalments should have an interest proportional to that required to pay the outstanding mortgage instalments.

This affirms the position taken in *Gissing v Gissing* that the proportions depend on common intention.

This raises problems in a negative equity situation.

Occupation and beneficial interests under a trust of land

Since the TLATA 1996 is now in force any beneficial interest lies in the land. Nevertheless the Trustees may still sell the land (see p 28) so that any purchaser overreaches the beneficiaries' interests in the land provided he or she pays the money to two trustees, ie the position is still in accordance with s 27 of the LPA 1925. The purchaser is not then concerned with the trust.

Where, however, one of the beneficiaries is in occupation of the property the position is more complicated. Under the new TLATA 1996 the trustees have absolute power to deal with the property unless the trust specifically prevents this, but the beneficial owners have a right of occupation under s 12 subject to the requirements of s 13. In the past, the courts have found interests of beneficiaries in occupation to be in more than the proceeds of sale.

In *Bull v Bull* (1955), a mother and son purchased a house together but the conveyance was in the sole name of the son. The son then married and subsequently gave his mother notice to quit. The court held the mother's beneficial interest under a trust for sale gave her a right of possession until such time as the house was sold, even though under the doctrine of conversion her interest was not in the property but only in money.

The TLATA 1996 now establishes that the mother's interest in such a case as a beneficiary under a trust of land is always in the property itself.

A difficulty may arise when one beneficiary under the trust wishes to sell while the other(s) does not. Section 12 of the TLATA 1996 gives equitable owners the right to occupy the property and allows for its exclusive use by one such owner with requisite compensation for the other and any such owner may also apply to the court under s 14 to prevent any sale of the property.

It remains to be seen whether s 12 will prevent the situation in *City of London v Flegg* (1988) where because the purchase money had been paid to two trustees as required by s 27 of the LPA 1925, the interests of two further trustees in occupation were overreached.

The position where land is registered seems to remain the same. The landmark case before the TLATA 1996 was *William and Glyn's Bank v Boland* (1987) where a husband and wife purchased a matrimonial home together but the legal title was in the husband's name only. The husband mortgaged the house without his wife's knowledge and then he defaulted, and the mortgagees sought possession of the house.

The court decided that the wife had a beneficial interest under a trust for sale. She was also in occupation and since the land was registered, her occupation gave her an overriding interest under s 70(g) of the Land Registration Act (LRA) 1925:

> The rights of every person in actual occupation of the land or in receipt of the rents and profits thereof, save where enquiry is made of such person and the rights are not disclosed.

This means that if the bank had asked the wife if she had any rights and she had not acknowledged that she had, then the bank would have taken the house, but the bank had not done so. Her occupation gave her an interest in the house itself and not merely in its value. (See *Kingsnorth Finance Co Ltd v Tizzard* (1986) for the position in unregistered land and the doctrine of notice in Chapter 1.)

In *Lloyd's Bank v Rosset* (1991), it was stated that 'actual occupation' is to be given its ordinary and plain meaning.

Note
State Bank of India v Soad (1997) establishes that it is not necessary for capital money to be actually paid to two trustees for overreaching to occur. Overreaching may take place when trustees 'use' the property, eg take out a charge on it, in which no money is paid.

Spouses and occupation

Even if a spouse does not have a beneficial interest in the matrimonial home he or she may have a right of occupation under the Matrimonial Homes Act (MHA) 1983. This gives the spouse the right not to be evicted or excluded by the other spouse without an ouster order from the court. As a statutory right of occupation it may be registered as a Class F land charge under the Land Charges Act (LCA) 1972 where the land is unregistered, but is not an overriding interest under s 70(1)(g) of the LRA 1925 in the case of registered land; it is only registrable by way of a notice 'as a minor interest'.

Note

This right is a purely personal right, not a right in land, it does not give any equity in land, but merely gives a spouse a right against the other spouse.

In such cases, the court will take into account all the circumstances of the case when asked to decide whether the purchaser or spouse should have precedence when one spouse wishes to sell.

In *Kashmir Kaur v Gill* (1988), the husband was in the process of selling the matrimonial house to a blind man. The wife had no beneficial interest in the house but applied to enter her right of occupation under the MHA 1983.

The court decided that all the circumstances could be taken into account. The blind person wanted to purchase the house because it was more convenient for him than his present home so the wife's application was not granted.

Under s 37 of the MPPA 1970 where a spouse makes a substantial contribution in money or money's worth to the improvement of the property in which either spouse or both has a beneficial interest, that spouse will be treated as having a share in a beneficial interest by virtue of that contribution, unless there is an express or implied agreement to the contrary (ie will have an interest in any proceeds from the sale of the property).

Be careful

The above acts apply to *spouses only* not to cohabitees.

Question hints

Questions on co-ownership and trusts for sale usually fall into two groups: those on joint tenancies and those on co-ownership where only one person holds the legal title.

Joint tenancies

Such questions usually involve the purchase of a property by several people who then 'disappear' by a series of events.

* Remember first, that any purchasers of property acting together are joint tenants under an 'implied' trust of land as laid down in the TLATA 1996 which amends s 34(2) of the LPA 1925. The legal title can still only be held as joint tenants. If there are more than four

purchasers, the first four only, can be trustees (s 34). Any remaining purchasers will not be trustees unless any of the first four are barred from being trustees because they are minors or legally incapable.

- Now consider how the equitable interests are held. Does the question quote the conveyance? Or is there some other indication, eg words indicating equal shares (ie words which suggest the equitable interests are held as tenants in common). If it is not clear, say so, and indicate the two possibilities. In such a case you will have to deal with all the events, both with the equitable interests held on a joint tenancy and held as tenants in common.

  Remember that equity leans against joint tenancies and consider the equitable presumptions, eg look for a partnership and indicate why it is important to know how the equitable interests are held, eg *jus accrescendi*.

- Go through each subsequent event in turn. Is there severance? Are there 'such other acts' (s 36(2) of the LPA 1925)? Do any of the facts in the question fit decided cases? (*Burgess v Rawnsley*). Is there a death involving a will? If so, remember that a clause leaving 'my realty to X' will have no meaning if the testator has no realty. If the testator died before 1 January 1997 the trust created by the will will be subject to the doctrine of conversion so the land held by him as a joint tenant will not be regarded as realty. After this date the interests of the beneficiaries will remain in realty, ie land.

- Stress each time that severance occurs the joint tenancy of the legal title is not affected and calculate how the beneficial interests are then held.

- You will probably find that severance has left you with two or three people, one of whom wants to sell. As trustees they now have absolute power. One or more of them may decide to approach the court under s 14 of the TLATA 1996 as an 'interested person'. Consider s 15 which states the order in which the court will look at the relevant facts. *Re Mayo* (1943) is authority that, in the case of a trust for sale, where trustees disagree there must be a sale, but remember the doctrine of conversion then applied.

- Finally calculate what each person will receive if there is a sale.

Co-ownership where only one person holds the legal title

Such questions usually involve a matrimonial home or cohabitees where the person holding the legal title does something (eg takes out a mortgage and then defaults) which results in a third party seeking possession of the property.

- Explain the problem, ie that the person not holding the legal title can only prevent possession if he or she can prove he or she (usually a man or woman situation) has a beneficial interest in the property. Then point out the difficulty that an interest in land can only be acquired by deed (s 52(1) of the LPA 1925 or by writing s 53(1)(a)) and in the absence of these the only recourse is to prove a resulting, implied or *constructive trust* so that s 53(2) of the LPA 1925 applies to give such an interest.
- Briefly indicate the confusion over terms (ie state that the words 'resulting trust' and 'constructive trust' have been used interchangeably), and stress, that in any case, for both a resulting and constructive trust there must be a common intention that there should be such a beneficial interest.
- Explain that in a resulting trust such common intention is demonstrated by a direct contribution to the purchase price either by deposit or to mortgage repayments but remember that a gift of money towards payment of purchase price or mortgage is not such a contribution by the donor.
- Explain the requirement of common intention for a constructive trust, and that this must be accompanied by some act which would not have been done by the person not holding the legal title, *if* there had not been a common intention that he or she would have a beneficial interest in the property. Such an act to one's detriment must be done in such belief of a common intention. Consider Lord Bridge's words in *Lloyd's Bank v Rosset*.
- Look at the facts of the problem before you. Is it analogous to cases such as *Grant v Edwards*? Be careful to point out any differences in the facts of your problem and the cases you refer to. Can you find an act to a detriment? Are the acts 'substantial' (*Pettit v Pettit*)? Would such acts satisfy *Lloyd's Bank v Rosset* or is the situation closer to *Burns v Burns*?
- Remember if there is a resulting or constructive trust then the legal title holder holds on a trust of land, so any sale of the property requires payment to two trustees (s 27 of the LPA 1925). Could the beneficial interest have been protected? Remember, if the land is unregistered and the person with the beneficial interest is in occupation the doctrine of notice applies (*Kingsnorth Finance v Tizard* (1986)).
- If it is registered then occupation (because of the beneficial interest) is an overriding interest under s 70(1)(g) of the LRA 1925.

41

Note

Such a question is often combined with undue influence where a mortgage is involved – then you must refer to *Barclays Bank v O'Brien* (see Chapter 9).

4 Settlements

You should be familiar with the following areas:

- strict settlements
- definition
- how strict settlements arise
- express creation
- the tenant for life
- problems
- settlements under a trust of land
- a comparison between the two types

Definition

A settlement is a disposition of property creating a succession of interests in it. It must be created by deed. Two types of settlement could be created before the new Trusts of Land and Appointment of Trustees Act (TLATA) 1996 came into force on 1 January 1997.

- a strict settlement governed by the Settled Land Act (SLA) 1925; and
- a trust for sale form of settlement governed by the Law of Property Act (LPA) 1925.

The TLATA 1996 abolished trusts for sale which have now become trusts of land as explained in Chapter 3.

Strict settlements created before 1 January 1997 continue but no more may be created for the purpose of conducting successive interests in land (s 2 of the TLATA 1996). Such pre-existing strict settlements are still governed by the SLA 1925.

How a strict settlement could have arisen

- By express creation.
- Inadvertently by a will which was not carefully worded.
- By statute. Where a person entitled to a legal estate was illegally capable of holding it, eg a minor or someone who was mentally disabled, under s 1(1)(ii)(d) of the SLA 1925 a strict settlement arose.
- By action of a court, eg *Binions v Evans* (1972).

The express creation of a strict settlement

By such words as: 'to X for life, then to Y for life, then to Z'. In such a case, X becomes the tenant for life with Y and Z having beneficial interests; when X and Y are dead Z takes absolutely.

Note
If the words 'on trust for sale' were included then there was no strict settlement, the settlement was one under a trust for sale and now becomes a trust of land. The two types of settlement, a strict settlement and a trust for sale were mutually exclusive. Remember that if the strict settlement was created before 1 January 1997 it is still extant and governed by the SLA 1925 as considered below.

Creation *inter vivos*

Section 4 of the SLA 1925 covers strict settlements created *inter vivos*. It requires *two* instruments:

- A vesting deed; transferring the legal estate to the tenant for life (unless the settler is himself the tenant for life, in which case the legal title remains vested in him).
- A trust instrument; this declares the terms of the trust and appoints trustees.

Note
If a settler makes a trust instrument but no vesting deed the settlement is incompletely constituted; no transfer will be deemed to have taken place and the legal estate remains with the settler. In this situation s 9 of the SLA 1925 allows the tenant for life to request the trustees to make a vesting deed.

Creation by will

Section 6 of the SLA 1925 covers the creation of a strict settlement by will. In this case:

- the will is deemed to be the trust instrument;
- there is no vesting deed; instead the testator's PRs make a vesting assent transferring the legal estate to the tenant for life.

Who is the tenant for life?

A tenant for life is defined in s 117(1)(xxviii) of the SLA 1925. In addition a tenant for life is:

- s 19(1): 'the person of full age who is for the time being beneficially entitled under a settlement to possession of settled land for the purposes of this Act';
- s 19(2): 'where two or more persons are so entitled, they together constitute the tenant for life'.

Where there is no tenant for life, eg where the persons so entitled are legally incapable of holding a legal estate (as in the case of minors and the mentally disabled), then the powers of the tenant for life fall to the *statutory owner* defined in s 117(1)(xxvi) as the trustees of the settlement or any person on whom such powers are conferred by the settlement.

Section 23 covers the powers of such persons where there is no tenant for life.

Note
There can be no tenant for life:

- Where rent is payable
  In *Re Catling* (1931), a widow was left property for life on payment of nominal rent of £1 per annum. It was held that she could not be a tenant for life if she paid rent.
- Where the whole estate is not vested in the tenant for life
  The following a cases illustrate this:
  Re Frewen (1926). A beneficiary was given only part of the income from settled land, the remainder was to be accumulated; he was deemed not to be a tenant for life because he was not entitled to the whole income from the land.
  Re Jeffreys (1939). A beneficiary was to be paid a fixed annuity out of the estate. He was deemed not to be a tenant for life because he was not entitled to the whole estate.

- Where the trustees are given discretion
  In *Re Gallenga* (1938), trustees were given power to decide whether or not to pay the beneficiary the income from the estate. It was held that this was not settled land but land under a discretionary trust.

The powers of the tenant for life

The most important powers of the tenant for life are contained in ss 38–42 and 71 of the SLA 1925, ie the power to sell, lease or mortgage the settled land. However, the powers conferred are limited by the following:

Section 101
This states that the tenant for life must give the trustees a notice in writing of at least one month if he intends to exercise any of these powers, but in practice a general notice usually suffices. He must also obtain the best price reasonably obtainable in all these transactions.

Section 107
This affirms that the tenant for life must act as a trustee for all the other beneficiaries and have regard to their interests.

Section 104
Section 104 means that no constraints can be put on the exercise of the powers of the tenant for life.

Section 65
This is an exception to s 104 in that where the settled land consists of a 'principal mansion house' consent is required:

- for a settlement made after 1 January 1926, where the settlement expressly states such consent is required;
- for a settlement made pre-1926 unless the settlement expressly states it is not.

A 'principal mansion house' is defined as exceeding 25 acres and not being a farmhouse.

Section 38: the power to sell

A tenant for life may sell the settled land but:
- If the tenant for life exercises his power to sell, the purchase money must be paid to two trustees s 18 of the SLA 1925. This means that the beneficial interests of others under the settlement are overreached

and become vested in the capital sum. The tenant for life receives the income from this capital sum, ie the purchase price.

- Section 39 requires any sale to be for the best price reasonably obtainable.

In *Wheelwright v Walker* (1883), land was settled on X for life with remainder to X's daughter. The daughter sold her beneficial interest to P so that P would become absolute owner when X died. X then decided, as tenant for life, to exercise her power to sell under s 38. P objected and sought an injunction to prevent sale.

The court did not order an injunction. Section 38 gave the tenant for life a right to sell.

P then found out that X was going to sell at a very low price and applied for an injunction to prevent such sale. An injunction was granted; X must sell in accordance with s 39 and obtain the best price she reasonably could.

- Where the tenant for life does sell the purchaser will take subject to any leases, easements and other rights existing under the settlement.

Note

If the tenant for life sells all the land after 1 January 1997, then under the new TLATA 1996, the strict settlement ceases and becomes a trust of land. If he only sells part of the settled land then the strict settlement remains in existence.

Sections 41 and 42: the power to grant leases

A tenant for life may lease his land to a lessee but such a lease is subject to the following restrictions:

- in the case of a building lease to 999 years;
- in the case of a mining lease to 100 years;
- in the case of a forestry lease to 999 years;
- in the case of any other lease to 50 years.

Section 71: the power to mortgage

Although a tenant for life may mortgage settled land, he may only do so subject to the following restrictions that:
- the money is payable to two trustees;
- a mortgage is only possible if the money is required for any of the following purposes:

(a) for *authorised* improvements. This does *not* mean repairs which must be paid for out of current income from the estate;

(b) to discharge existing encumbrances on the land;

(c) for equality of exchange where an exchange of property is being made;

- the mortgage must be a legal mortgage.

Note
The tenant for life can, of course, mortgage his own beneficial interest but this will be an equitable mortgage, not a legal one (see Chapter 10).

Problems arising from these powers of the tenant for life

Section 13 of the SLA 1925: 'the paralysing section'

This section makes any purported disposition of the legal estate an estate contract only until the estate has been vested in the tenant for life by a vesting deed or assent. Until the settlement is completely constituted and there is a vesting deed or assent, there can be no disposition. If there is only a trust instrument the settlement is incompletely constituted.

Note
If the settlement is by will the personal representatives are able to sell the land without a vesting deed.

The problem of s 18 and s 110

Section 18 requires any purchase money to be paid to two trustees and states that any disposition *by the tenant for life* (ie where legal estate has been vested in him) shall be void unless it is made in conformity with the requirements of the Act.

Section 110(2) contains the *curtain principal* and prevents any prospective purchaser from seeing the trust instrument. He can see the vesting instrument and from this *should* be able to assume the person in whom the land is vested is the tenant for life or statutory owner having the power thereby to make a sale of the settled land.

Section 110(1) makes it clear that where a purchaser *deals with a tenant for life* or statutory owner in good faith he will take, even if the requirements of s 18 are not met.

The problem arises where the purchaser deals with someone who purports to be an absolute owner but is, in fact, a tenant for life. There are two conflicting cases on this issue.

In *Weston v Henshaw* (1950), a father conveyed property to his son in fee simple absolute. His son later conveyed it back to him but kept the original conveyance deed. The father later made a will creating a settlement whereby his son became a life tenant and his grandson the remainderman. The father died and his son became life tenant and the legal title was vested in him. This son then mortgaged the property but used the original conveyance deed to obtain the mortgage, ie he purported to be the absolute owner. He then died and the remainderman who was the grandson claimed the property against the claim of the mortgagee.

The court held that the mortgagee was not a *bona fide* purchaser for valuable consideration dealing in good faith within s 110(1). He had not dealt with the father as a tenant for life, he had dealt with him as an absolute owner. He did not know he was dealing with settled land.

In *Re Morgan's Lease* (1970), on the other hand, it was held that s 110(1) did apply to any purchaser who acted in good faith whether or not he knew he was dealing with settled land.

Since neither case has precedence because both are only first instance the weight of opinion is that *Re Morgan's Lease* is the better decision.

Note

For strict settlements arising from the action of a court, eg *Binion v Evans* (1972), see Chapter 7.

Settlements under a trust of land

In Chapter 3, it was emphasised that a trust of land was created where there was co-ownership and concurrent interests, but a settlement, ie a disposition involving successive interests can also be created by the express words 'trust of land' in an instrument.

All settlements created since 1 January 1997 are trusts of land and are governed by the TLATA 1996.

Examples

'My freehold estate Blackacre, to John on trust of land for life, then to Belinda for life, remainder to Andrew', creates a settlement.

'Whiteacre to Emily and Edward as trustees to hold on trust of land for David for life, then to Alice absolutely' creates a settlement.

Comparison of a strict settlement and a settlement under a trust of land

Formation
Both may be created by express words. This is usually the case but a strict settlement can have been created by accident, eg by a badly worded will.

Governing Act
For a strict settlement it is the SLA 1925; for a trust of land, the TLATA 1996. No more strict settlements under the SLA 1925 may be created.

Mode of creation
A strict settlement required two documents, a vesting deed and a trust instrument if it was created *inter vivos* under s 4 of the SLA 1925; or the will as the trust instrument and a vesting assent (created by the personal representatives) if the settlement was created by will under s 6 of the SLA 1925. A trust of land under a settlement requires a trust instrument.

The legal estate
In a strict settlement, the legal estate is vested in the tenant for life or statutory owner (where the tenant for life is a minor or there is no tenant for life) (s 19 of the SLA 1925). However, in a trust of land, the legal estate is vested in the trustees as it was under a trust for sale except that now the trustees have an absolute power with no duty to sell.

Powers of dealing with the estate
In a strict settlement, the tenant for life has power to sell, lease or mortgage the estate (ss 38–42 and s 71 of the SLA 1925).

In a trust of land, the trustees have absolute power unless the trust declares otherwise (see Chapter 3).

Restriction on powers
The only restrictions on the powers of the tenant for life are those governing how he may sell, lease or mortgage the estate; he or she cannot be prevented from doing any of these acts (s 106 of the LPA 1925).

In a trust of land, the settlor can restrict the powers of the trustees by inserting clauses requiring consents.

The capital money
When an estate is sold the purchase money becomes capital money and in both types of settlement it must be paid to two trustees.

In the strict settlement, there may be a maximum of four trustees, in which case all four must sign the receipt for the money (s 27(2) of the SLA 1925). Such capital money must be invested and the tenant for life is only entitled to the income from it.

In the trust of land the money is paid to two trustees (s 27 of the LPA 1925).

The beneficiaries

In a strict settlement, the beneficiaries have no power to prevent the tenant for life from selling the estate. If he or she does so, provided the money is paid to two trustees, their interests are overreached and become vested in the capital sum. He or she is required to give notice of an intention to sell to the trustees but not to the beneficiaries but, as trustee of their interests, he or she should give due consideration to their interests.

In a trust of land, the interests of the beneficiaries are in the land itself and the trustees are required to consult all the beneficiaries as to their wishes if they are considering selling.

Under s 106 of the SLA 1925, a beneficiary under a strict settlement cannot prevent sale but under a trust for land a beneficiary may, 'as a person interested' apply to the court under s 14 of the TLATA 1996 for an order that the trustees shall sell or not sell.

The trustees

The trustees under a strict settlement must vest the legal estate in the tenant for life, and should he or she die, in the next person so entitled, until only the remainderman is left. They must then execute a discharge deed (s 17 of the SLA 1925). Their other duties are limited.

The trustees under a trust of land have absolute power unless the instrument curtails it.

5 Easements and profits *à prendre*

> **You should be familiar with the following areas:**
>
> - definition
> - characteristics
> - creation
> - easements of light
> - legal and equitable easements and third parties
> - extinguishment of easements
> - the Right of Access to Neighbouring Land Act 1992

Definitions

An easement is a right over the land belonging to another person. A profit *à prendre* is a right to remove something from land belonging to another.

Characteristics of an easement

If a right is to be capable of being an easement it must satisfy the four conditions of *Re Ellenborough Park* (1956).

1. There must be a dominant and servient tenement
There must be a dominant tenement to benefit from the easement and a servient tenement over which the easement is exercised. There can be no easement if there is no dominant tenement.

2. The dominant and servient tenements must have different owners
This is because a person cannot have a right over his own land. If the dominant and servient tenements become owned by the same person, the easement ceases to exist.

3. The easement must accommodate the dominant tenement

The easement must confer a benefit on the dominant tenement. The benefit must be to the dominant tenement itself and not personal to the landowner (*Hill v Tupper* (1863)). This means the easement must increase the value of the dominant tenement or make it more saleable or benefit the dominant land in some other way. There must also be some nexus between the two tenements but they need not lie next to one another.

4. The easement must be capable of being the subject matter of a grant

There are four elements to this requirement:

- there must be a capable grantor;
- there must be a capable grantee, ie a person entitled to make the grant;
- the easement must be capable of being described with certainty. *Voice v Bell* (1993) illustrates this element. An easement of a right of way was not granted where the land to be benefited over which the right of way was claimed was merely described as land at the rear of the property. It was not clear whether there was any land capable of being benefited by a right of way;
- the right is already recognised as being capable of being an easement.

Examples of rights which have been regarded as capable of being easements

- A right of access.
- A right to park vehicles (*London and Blenheim Estates Ltd v Ladbroke Retail Parks Ltd* (1993)). *Per curiam*: the right to park cars is capable of being an easement provided it is in relation to the area over which it is granted. This means it is not such as would leave the servient owner without any reasonable use of his land.
- A right of support of a dividing wall of a shared building (ie party wall) (*Bradburn v Lindsay* (1983)). However, there is no right of protection from the weather if a party wall of a house is exposed (*Phipps v Pears* (1965)) (though there may be protection under s 29(5) of the Public Health Act 1961 which allows a Local Authority to require weatherproofing).

Examples of rights which have not been regarded as being capable of being easements

- Rights which impose expenditure on the servient tenement owner.

Exception

The right to have a fence or wall between neighbouring properties in good repair has been held to be in the nature of an easement (*Crow v Wood* (1971)).

The right to have common areas maintained; eg entrance, stairs, lifts is capable of being an easement (*Liverpool City Council v Irwin* (1977)).

- Rights which amount to a claim for joint user.
  In the case of *Grisby v Melville* (1974), the only access to a cellar was held not to be capable of being an easement since it required going through an adjoining cellar of another's property. It was a claim for joint user.

A claim to storage was held to be one of a joint user and so not capable of being an easement in *Copeland v Greenhalf* (1952).

- A right to privacy (*Browne v Flower* (1911)).
- A right to a view (*Aldred's* case).
- A right to a general flow of air.

But

New easements can still be capable of being recognised. In *Dyce v Lady James Hay* (1852) Lord St Leonards stated:

> The category of easements must alter and expand with the changes that take place in the circumstances of mankind.

This means that changing social conditions may give rise to new easements being acknowledged by the courts.

The creation of easements

Even if a purported right is capable of being an easement, it still has to be created. Easements may be created in four ways: by express grant or reservation; implied grant or reservation; by s 62 of the Law of Property Act (LPA) 1925; by prescription.

Express grant or reservation

An express grant is by deed or will with express words giving an easement to the owner of the dominant tenement. It is given by the owner of the servient tenement.

A reservation is where the owner of land sells part of it and retains the rest expressly reserving an easement for the land he retains, ie he or she creates the retained land as the dominant tenement and the land he or she sells as the servient tenement.

Implied grant or reservation

There are two types of such easements and one quasi-easement created in this way.

Implied easements of necessity

This is where the court is willing to find an easement because without it the land cannot be enjoyed at all (*Nickerson v Barraclough* (1981)).

Implied by common intention at the time of the conveyance

This was illustrated by *Wong v Beaumont Property Trust Ltd* (1965) where a basement was purchased for use as a restaurant at the time of sale. This was an express understanding. Such use required adequate ventilation, this was, at the time, also known at time of sale (and necessitated fixing a duct to the outside walls although this was not then known).

The court held that there was an implied intention of an easement of necessity. It was not possible to use other means of ventilation, therefore, the duct must be allowed.

In *Stafford v Lee* (1993), the plaintiffs were only able to reach their land over the defendant's road. The plaintiffs wanted to build a house on this land which was woodland, so claimed an implied easement to reach it because of a common intention that they should have access. The defendant claimed, if there was an implied easement, it was only to the woodland as woodland, not for the purposes of development.

It was held that if the parties to a grant of land had a common intention about how the land should be used, which in this case they had and if that intention could not be carried out without the easement claimed (it could not) then the easement would be implied.

Note

This differs from *Wong v Beaumont* in that the land could still be used, ie as woodland, so there was no strict necessity for the easement: the restaurant in *Wong* could not have been used without the duct.

Quasi-easement implied under the rule in *Wheeldon v Burrows* (1879)

This allows a quasi-easement based on the principle that a grantor may not derogate from his grant, so that on a conveyance something in the nature of an easement is created for a right previously existing. This kind of easement needs to be:

* A right which is 'continuous and apparent'.

  A right used for a substantial period of time so it can be seen or discovered, eg a well-worn path. It does not have to be conspicuous

but discoverable on 'a careful inspection by a person ordinarily conversant with the subject'.
• Necessary to the *reasonable* enjoyment of the land.

Note
There is some confusion as to whether 'continuous and apparent' and 'necessary to reasonable enjoyment' are alternatives or whether both are required. The former seems to be the majority view.

• A right must have been in use at the time of the conveyance.

Always
When using *Wheeldon v Burrows* make sure:

• there has been a transfer of some kind, eg an oral lease;
• the vendor has retained the servient land *at the time* of sale (even if he sells it later).

The rule was used in *Borman v Griffith* (1930), a case that involved a private park in which were two properties 'The Gardens' and 'The Hall'.

The owner leased 'The Gardens' to X. 'The Gardens' was reached by a drive leading off a drive to 'The Hall'. No other access was possible so in effect 'The Garden' was a dominant tenement benefited by the drive as a right of access.

The owner then leased 'The Hall' (the retained servient tenement) to Y who tried to prevent X using the drive.

The court decided that an easement of access existed. It satisfied the requirement of *Wheeldon v Burrows*.

The recent case of *Wheeler v Saunders* (1995) illustrates the limits of *Wheeldon v Burrows*.

A house and farmland were owned by the same owner. There was a road to the house but it could also be reached by going across the farmland. Then the house and farmland were sold but to different persons. There was no grant of a right of way over the farmland to the house and the owner of the farmland refused to allow the owner of the house to reach it across the farmland. The owner of the house argued that there was an implied easement under the rule in *Wheeldon v Burrows*.

It was held that *Wheeldon v Burrows* requires that the implied easement be necessary for the reasonable enjoyment of the property and in use at the time of the grant. Here there was no such necessity; there was another means of access and no implied easement.

In *Millman v Ellis* (1996), it was stressed that *Wheeldon v Burrows* meant that all those implied continuous and apparent easements necessary for the reasonable enjoyment of the land, used at the time of the grant by the owner of the land, pass to the purchaser. If an owner wishes to preserve any right he has, he must reserve it expressly in the grant.

By s 62 of the LPA 1925

Section 62 implies into all conveyances (unless a contrary intention is expressed), 'all ... privileges, easements, rights and advantages whatsoever appertaining to the land at the time of the conveyance'. This means a mere personal privilege can become an easement.

Note

There must be a conveyance by deed. In *Wright v Macadam* (1949) Mrs M was allowed to store coal in her landlord's shed in the garden of the property she rented. One year later she took a new lease on the property. It contained no mention of the shed. The landlord then tried to charge for use of the shed.

It was held that the new lease was a conveyance within s 62 of the LPA 1925. There was no contrary intention contained in the lease so she had acquired a legal easement.

Be careful to distinguish between:

One property	Two separate properties	
House and land leased by Mrs Macadam Shed belonging to Mr Wright	Landlord's property and shed **Whiteacre** Shed used by X for storage	**Blackacre** Land leased from landlord by X

(a) Mr Wright's shed was on Mrs M's property before her lease renewal; but the shed is in Mrs Macadam"s garden and both shed and property are owned by Mr Wright. Mrs M obtains an easement of storage in the shed under the conveyance (s 62 of the LPA 1925) because she had used the shed for storage before the conveyance.

(b) X used the shed on his landlord's land, Whiteacre, for storage and then renews the lease on land he previously leased, ie Blackacre. He does *not* obtain easement of storage because the shed is not on *his* land but on Whiteacre retained by the landlord. He is trying to claim joint user.

Prescription

All forms of prescription require three conditions:

- User as of right: that is *nec vi* (without force), *nec clam* (without secrecy), *nec precario* (without permission).

  In *Diment v NH Foot Ltd* (1974), it was held that there was no easement of a right of way because the owner would not have known of such use since it was never reported to her by those responsible for the land, so it was not *nec clam* ...

- A right by one fee simple owner against another.
  There can be no prescription under a lease (*Kilgner v Geddes* (1904)).

- User must be continuous.
  This does not mean it cannot be interrupted. *Mills v Silver* (1991) held that the use must be such that as to a reasonable person it would be considered that a continuous right (in this case to use a path) is being asserted and the owner who must thereby know this, does nothing. Toleration of a user by the owner is deemed to be consent or acquiescence.
  A variation in a right of way agreed between the servient and dominant land owners does not negate a continuous user (*Davis v Whitby* (1973)).

If and *only* if the above three requirements are met can prescription be obtained by either common law, the fiction of the lost modern grant or the Prescription Act (PA) 1832.

By the common law
This means by long user from *time immemorial*, ie from 1189. This is rebuttable by showing:

- the user could not have been in existence at that date;
- that at some date since then, the dominant and servient tenements had come under the same ownership.

But if these two conditions cannot be shown, proof that the right has existed for 20 years suffices, provided the conditions for all forms of prescription are met.

The fiction of the lost modern grant
This requires:

- a grant made after 1189 but the deed has been lost;
- a 20 year user.

The presumption is rebutted by proof that such a grant could never have been made because no one legally could have made it.

In *Re St Martin Le Grand York* (1989) a path over a burial ground was claimed as an easement of a right of way. It was held that there was no prescription by the fiction of lost modern grant. No such grant was possible over a church burial ground.

The Prescription Act 1832

Remember you must satisfy the three conditions of all methods of acquiring an easement by prescription first, but user as of right is defeated for the purposes of prescription under the PA 1832 if:

- it has been by permission at any time during the periods of use prescribed by the act; *and*
- written permission was given when user began; *or*
- oral permission was given when user began for the shorter period.

Oral permission when user began for the longer period will not defeat a claim under the act.

The statutory periods for claims under the PA 1832

The shorter period

Twenty years for easements and 30 years for profits *à prendre*. If such a period of use can be shown, a claim to an easement at common law cannot be defeated by showing it commenced after 1189, ie from time immemorial.

The longer period

Forty years for easements and 60 years for profits *à prendre*. Such a period makes a claimed right, absolute and indefeasible, unless there is written proof (a deed or agreement) that consent has been given.

Note

There are deductions for each period (ss 2 and 7 of the PA 1832):
- For the shorter period when the servient owner is:
  (a) an infant;
  (b) a patient under the Mental Health Act;
  (c) a tenant for life;
- For the longer period only when the servient owner is a tenant for life.

Those periods for deductions are subtracted from the total period of user.

Example

Blackacre is settled land. The tenant for life enjoyed it from 1 January 1970 to 31 December 1980. His son inherited absolutely as remainder-man on 1 January 1981 when he was two years old. He died in June 1983 and was succeeded by his uncle who became senile and was a patient in a mental hospital until January 1986 when he died. The present owner is of full age and competent.

X has a right of way over Blackacre. He is claiming as:

20 year user

X must deduct 10 years for ownership by the original tenant for life; two and a half years for ownership by a minor, ie his son, and two and a half years for ownership by a mental patient.

A total of 15 years is to be deducted.

X will have to establish user from 1994 – (15 + 20) = 1959.

40 year user

Only 10 years deduction. X will have to establish user from 1994 – (10 + 40) = 1944.

Note

The 20 year and 40 year periods are deemed to be next before action, ie before a claim is bought, the enjoyment of the right must be immediately before the action.

Easement of light: s 3 of the PA 1932

The main features of this are:

- a period of 20 years enjoyment of light without interruption is deemed absolute and indefeasible. There is no other period but 20 years;
- the user need not be 'as of right' provided it is not by a written agreement;
- the right is not limited to owners in fee simple. A tenant can acquire an easement of light against his landlord;
- there are no deductions.

What can a servient owner do to prevent an easement of light?

- Block off light so the easement cannot be established but this may bring him into conflict with local planning laws.

- Register a notice as a local land charge under the Rights to Light Act 1959. The notice must specify the position and size of a notional obstruction and state the dominant and servient tenements. If the dominant tenement owner does not object within a year, then there will be deemed an interruption to the right to light.

The amount of light

The criterion in questions of loss of light is 'is there a sufficient amount' of light? (not how much light is lost).

The test was established in *Collis v Home and Colonial Stores* (1904) as sufficient for the beneficial use of premises in the case of business premises and, for comfortable use in case of a dwelling house. The rule is the 50/50 one, ie more than 50% of the area receives one lumen.

Greenhouses

Light must be sufficient for the growth of plants (*Allen v Greenwood* (1979)). In effect, this case created a new easement for a greenhouse and illustrates that the categories are not closed. (See Lord St Leonard's statement *above*, p 59.)

Legal and equitable easements and third parties

Easements may be legal or equitable.

Legal easements

Legal easements must be created by deed, statute or prescription. They must be held for an interest equivalent to an estate in fee simple in possession or for a term of years absolute (s 1(2)(a) of the LPA 1925).

If an easement does not satisfy *both* these conditions, it can only be an equitable easement.

As a right *in rem* a legal easement is:

- in unregistered land good against the whole world;
- in registered land an *overriding* interest under s 70(1)(a) of the Land Registration Act (LRA) 1925.

Equitable easements

In the case of registered land an equitable easement is a minor interest protected by notice or caution on the register.

Problem
Celsteel Ltd v Alton Holdings Ltd (1985) suggests an equitable easement may come within s 70(1)(a) of the LRA 1925 as an overriding interest where land is registered.

In the case of unregistered land, an equitable easement is registrable as a Class D(ii) land charge under the Land Charge Act (LCA) 1972, if it has been created after 1925. If it is not registered it is void against a purchaser of the legal estate for valuable consideration (*Shiloh Spinners Limited v Harding* (1973)).

For easements created pre-1925 the *doctrine of notice* applies (*Soames-Forsythe Properties v Tesco* (1991)). This is so whether the land is registered or unregistered.

Extinguishment of easements

Easements may be extinguished by:

Statute

Merger
When the dominant and servient tenements come under the same ownership the easement is extinguished, but if there is single owner-ship yet different occupation, the easement is not lost for ever. If the dominant and servient tenements subsequently come under different owners the easement will be resurrected.

Release
There are two ways of extinguishing an easement by release:
- by express release, ie by deed or express release without deed (oral or written) and estoppel;
- by implied release by 20 year non-user. This is sufficient to raise the presumption of abandonment but is rebuttable by proof of non-intention to abandon (*Moore v Rawson* (1824)).

The Right of Access to Neighbouring Land Act 1992

The Right of Access to Neighbouring Land Act 1992 is an attempt to marry two conflicting concepts:

- the traditional view of an Englishman's home as his castle; and
- public interest in the maintenance of housing standards.

Note

Access is defined as 'being for basic preservation works', ie not for improvements or extensions.

Under s 2(4), a neighbour can charge, having regard to all the circumstances of the case as is 'just and reasonable'. This includes:
- the likely financial advantage to person seeking access;
- the inconvenience likely to be caused to the neighbour.

Section 2(5) gives the calculation to be used.

Section 4(1) makes the neighbour and his successors in title to his servient land bound by an access order, so that should he or she die or move, the order remains in force, but for the period stated only.

Section 5 amends the LCA 1972 and the LRA 1925 to give effect to this act.

Section 49(1)(j) of the LPA 1925 makes such an order a right or interest which can be protected by notice on the register.

Question hints

- Always ask first; could this be an easement?, that is, does it satisfy the four requirements of *Re Ellenborough Park*?
- If it does, has it been created? Do not go through all the methods of creation. If there is no express or implied grant or reservation, or any conveyance, merely say so and concentrate on prescription.
- If there is a conveyance is it by deed? If so s 62 of the LPA 1925 will apply. Remember *Wheeldon v Burrows* requires the same person to own or occupy what will become the dominant and servient tenements but does not require a deed, only a transfer of land.
- If it can only be prescription remember, that all three forms of prescription require fee simple owners and that there must be user as of right.

In all questions be careful to *use* cases. Look for similarities and differences between the facts of your problem and the case you consider relevant and evaluate what you think a court would decide.

- Whom are you advising? The person claiming an easement will want to know what he can do if you find he has one. Similarly, the person trying to prevent the exercise of the right will want to know, if you discover there is no easement, what he can do.
- Does the right need protecting? Equitable easements will need to be protected; remember the doctrine of notice applies if they are created pre-1925, afterwards protection is by Class D(iii) land charge if the land is unregistered. In registered land, they are overriding interests and so require no registration, on the authority of *Celsteel Ltd v Alton Holdings Ltd* (1985).

6 Leases

You should be familiar with the following areas:

- requirements
- types
- determination
- leasehold covenants and their enforceability
- sub-tenants
- implied covenants
- leasehold reform

Definition

A legal lease, ie a 'term of years absolute', is one of the two legal estates (s 1(1) of the Law of Property Act (LPA) 1925).

Section 205 (xxvii) of the LPA 1925 states that a term of years absolute means 'terms of years' and in this definition the expression 'terms of years' includes a term of less than a year, or for a year, or years and a fraction of a year or from year to year. This is why a weekly tenancy is a lease.

Requirements of a lease

There are four requirements for a lease.

1. There must be a term of years certain

Provided the term is certain the lease can be of any length. This means the date of the commencement of the lease and its determination must be known.

In *Lace v Chantler* (1944), an agreement for the duration of the war was held not to be for a term certain. There was no lease.

In *Prudential Assurance Co Ltd v London Residuary Body* (1992), the House of Lords affirmed *Lace v Chantler* in that the date at which the lease is to start must be certain before the lease takes effect.

The LPA 1925 has brought the following three types of leases within this requirement.

Reversionary leases: s 149(3)

A reversionary lease is one which is deferred, ie is to commence at a later date, but s 149(3) of the LPA 1925 states that a lease at a rent or a fine to commence more than 21 years after it has been granted is void. Similarly, a contract for a lease *to commence* more than 21 years later is void but a contract *to grant* a lease 21 years after the contract is made is valid.

Leases for lives or on marriage: s 149(6)

A lease for lives or on marriage becomes converted into a lease for a fixed term of 90 years determinable on the death or marriage of the original lessee or the survivor of such, but such leases must be at rent, or in consideration of a fine. Such leases may be determined before 90 years on one month's notice of the death or marriage of the lessee. If no rent or fine is required the land becomes settled land and there is no lease.

Examples

A lease to X for 100 years determinable on X's earlier death is still a lease for 90 years, because it is a lease for a life.

A lease to Y for 50 years, if she remains a spinster, is still a lease for 90 years but is determinable if, and when, Y marries.

Perpetually renewable leases

Leases which contain clauses allowing the lessee to renew the lease every time the lease expires are called perpetually renewable leases. They are converted by s 145 into leases for 2,000 years.

In *Caerphilly Concrete Products Ltd v Owen* (1972), an option to renew a lease for a further five years on the same terms as the original five year lease was construed as a perpetually renewable lease.

However, the courts are modifying earlier attitudes to such leases. In *Marjorie Burnett Ltd v Barclay* (1980), a clause in the lease allowed the leasee to renew the lease for a further seven years at a rent to be agreed and the lease so renewed was to contain a like covenant for a further term of seven years. The court held that the term thereby granted was a lease for three terms of seven years each. The court would only construe a clause so as to create a perpetually renewable lease if it contained an express obligation to this effect.

Note
A periodic tenancy is a lease where the fixed term in each period can be a week, a month, a year, ie a short period depending on how the rent is to be paid.

2. Formalities

There are certain formalities required for the creation of a lease. Leases may be created as legal leases or equitable leases.

The creation of legal leases by express grant
Section 52(1) of the LPA 1925 states that 'all conveyances of land or any interest therein are void for the purpose of conveying or creating a legal estate unless made by deed'.

But
Section 52(2) of the LPA 1925 states s 52(1): 'does not apply to leases or tenancies ... not required by law to be in writing'. This brings a lease for less than three years, created informally, within a legal lease. In addition, s 54(2) of the LPA 1925 states that nothing in the foregoing provisions of this Part of the Act shall affect the creation by parol of leases taking effect in possession for a term not exceeding three years at the best rent which can be reasonably obtained without taking a fine. A parol lease is a lease created orally.

Note
- There must be rent for such parol leases.
- The Act includes periodic tenancies.
- A term of three years requires a deed; this means a parol lease must be for a term of less than three years.
- Even if the lease has been created as a parol lease any assignment of it requires a deed in accordance with s 52 of the LPA 1925.

In *Crago v Julian* (1992), a husband and wife decided to divorce. The husband was a tenant under a legal lease created orally. The husband moved out stating that he transferred his lease to his wife. However, the landlord was not told. When the landlord found out he refused to accept rent from the wife, ordered her to quit and sought possession. The wife had spent money on improvements in the belief that she held the lease.

It was held that possession order should be given; there had been no assignment of the lease by deed so the wife had never been the tenant.

Creation of legal leases by implied grant

Section 55(c) of the LPA 1925 states that nothing in ss 53 and 54 shall affect the right to acquire an interest in land by virtue of taking possession. This means conduct can create a legal lease provided:

* rent is paid;
* consent to take possession was given.

This makes a periodic tenancy a legal lease even though other formalities are not met and even if it lasts more than three years.

The creation of equitable leases

These are usually created by accident, eg where there is a contract for a lease for more than three years but no deed, as in the case of an estate contract. In this situation, there must be a valid contract, so that if the contract was made before 26 September 1989, it must have been manifested and provided in writing (s 40 of the LPA 1925). If made after that date it must be in writing in accordance with s 2 of the Law of Property (Miscellaneous Provisions) Act 1989.

Such a contract is void at law but a court may enforce it in equity provided the equitable maxims are complied with, and may grant specific performance.

3. A term of years less than that of the grantor

This is required so that at the end of the term any sub-lease will revert to the lessee before the lessee's lease reverts to the landlord.

4. Exclusive possession

If there is no exclusive possession, there cannot be a lease, only a licence. This means there will be no protection against possession under the Rent Acts 1977 or Housing Act 1988.

The landmark case of *Street v Mountford* (1985) established that a lease requires exclusive possession at a rent. The title of an agreement 'licence' and the clause allowing the landlord 'at all times to enter the room' for certain purposes was held to be a sham, it did not represent the true intention of the parties. There was a lease not a licence.

Lord Templeman doubted whether there could be a licence if the occupant was anything less than a lodger and stressed that the determining factor is the intention of the parties at the time the agreement is made. Subsequent cases have built on this.

In *Antoniades v Villiers* (1988), cohabitees shared a one-bedroomed flat. The agreements were identical for each and contained the following:

- the title 'licence';
- the occupant is not to have any exclusive possession;
- the landlord is entitled at any time to use the room together with the licensee and is able to permit other persons to use all the rooms together with the licencees;
- the real intention is to create a licence which does not come within the Rent Acts.

The court held that:

- the cohabitees lived in a one-bedroomed flat and shared a bed. No one could ever have believed the landlord would ever have sought to share it;
- the landlord knew they were cohabitees; he really intended to create a joint tenancy;
- neither the occupants nor the landlord could show they were never to have exclusive possession;
- the agreement, therefore, was a sham; they had a lease.

In *AG Securities v Vaughan* (1988), a four-bedroomed flat was occupied by four people. Each had an agreement termed a licence for six months without the right to exclusive possession of any part of the flat. Rents were different but there was in each agreement a provision that, if anyone left, a replacement was to be by mutual agreement.

The court decided that they had licences only: the agreements were between the landlord and the individual tenants, there was no joint occupancy so there could be no joint tenancy.

In *Aslan v Murphy* (1989), the agreement of an occupant of a one-roomed flat allowed the 'licensor':

- to use the rooms only at a specified time;
- no right of exclusive possession to any part of this one room; and
- stated the landlord could permit others to use the room and he himself had a right of entry at all times and a right to retain the keys.

The court reviewed the previous cases and emphasised the need to consider whether the agreement was a sham. If it was not, it was possible some clauses in it could be. This was so in the case of the clauses restricting the times the room could be used and its use by others.

Note

The retention of keys by the landlord in this case was held to be of no significance; a landlord could need the keys for a variety of reasons.

In *Skipton Building Society v Clayton* (1993), a couple, B and his wife, owned a leasehold flat. They conveyed it to Clayton at a price less than that of the market price. In return, Clayton gave them a licence to remain in the flat. Clayton then sought a mortgage. In order to get one, he asked B to sign a document in which the B and his wife gave up any interest in the flat. B did so and forged his wife's signature on the document. The mortgagee building society sent a surveyor to the flat who reported that, although it was furnished, there was no-one living there. In return for the document, Clayton gave the couple a new licence of the flat for life.

Clayton then defaulted on the mortgage repayments and the building society sought possession. B and his wife argued that they had a tenancy and, therefore, that their occupation gave them an overriding interest under s 70(1)(g) of the Land Registration Act (LRA) 1925.

The building society claimed that:

- they only had a licence;
- even if they had a tenancy, they had impliedly consented to the mortgage (citing *Abbey National Building Society v Cann*).

The court held that:
- The couple had exclusive possession; the agreements and re-licences were both shams so they did have an interest which their actual occupation made an overriding one under s 70(1)(g) of the LRA 1925. They had a lease for life which under s 149(6) of the LPA 1925 became a lease for 90 years. The lower price they received when they sold the flat to Clayton served as the fine required by s 149(6).
- There was no implied consent. Mrs B knew nothing about the mortgage and in Mr B's case there was no consent either; he knew about the mortgage but he did not consent to its having priority over his interest.

Exclusive possession without a lease, only a licence

In certain cases, an occupier may have exclusive possession but still not have a lease, only a licence.

This was considered in *Errington v Errington and Woods* (1952) which referred to exclusive possession, and found there were exceptions where such exclusive possession did not create a lease. These occur mainly where there have been informal arrangements and no intention to create legal relations.

Such exceptions now come with the category of 'Facchini' exceptions (from the *Facchini v Bryson* (1952) case) and include exceptions involving the following categories:

- *Family arrangements, acts of kindness, etc*
  These are where there is no intention to create legal relations, eg where there are no formal arrangements about payment of rent.
  In *Bostock v Bryant* (1991), a family was allowed to occupy a house on the condition that they paid the fuel bills. It was held that they had a licence only; there was no fixed rent.

- *Occupation accompanying service*
  Where exclusive possession is associated with employment there may or may not be a lease.
  In *Norris v Checkfield* (1992), it was held that if occupation was for purposes of work only, then there was only a licence and no lease.
  The test is; does the accommodation ensure better performance of duties? For instance, it need not be essential that such accommodation is provided, but if it is, it must increase work performance.
  In *Hughes v Mayor and Burgesses of LB of Greenwich* (1992), a headmaster's contract for a house in the school grounds included free board and lodging, but there was no express provision that he occupied the house for the better performance of his duties. He claimed a right to buy under the Housing Act 1985. He could not do this if he were a mere licensee.
  It was held that the house was not for the better performance of his duties, therefore, he had a tenancy not a licence and could buy.

- *Local Authorities and hostels*
  Recent cases suggest where private landlords have been deemed to have granted tenancies, local authorities may be considered to have granted only a licence.
  The basis of such cases appears to be (in the case of long-stay hostels which the residents regard as home):
  (a)   that there is normally a housekeeper living on the premises;
  (b)   there are rules residents must conform to, as in hostel licence.
  In *Westminster City Council v Clarke* (1992), the occupant of a single room in a hostel had sleeping and cooking facilities but he shared a bathroom. (This does not negate exclusive possession – see Chapter 7.)
  It was held that he was a licensee only. The hostel was for those with personality disorders so that rearrangement was often necessary if

an occupant destroyed a room. It was because of this need for flexibility that the court ruled he was more akin to a lodger and stated that the case was 'special' and should not be used as a precedent.

- *Residential homes*
  In *Abbeyfield v Harpenden Soc v Woods* (1968), a private organisation let rooms to senior citizens. Rent was paid weekly. The occupants were required to be self-sufficient and to leave when they required care.
  It was held that they were lodgers, and as such, only licencees.

The determination of tenancies (ie how tenancies may be terminated)

- By expiry of term, but this can be overruled, as for example in residential tenancies protected by the Rent Act 1977 and the Housing Act 1988. Notice of determination is not required unless specifically stated in the lease.
- By surrender of lease to the landlord and the landlord accepts it.
- By merger, ie both lease and landlord's reversion are held by the same person.
- By notice to quit. *Centaploy Ltd v Matlodge Ltd* (1974) affirmed a periodic tenancy cannot include a term preventing a landlord from giving notice to quit.
- If a tenant gives notice to quit then any sub-tenant to whom he or she may have leased the property must also quit (*Pennel v Payne* (1995)). This Court of Appeal case changes the law, but if a tenant surrenders his or her lease then his or her sub-tenant is not required to leave the property.

The date of determination was considered in *Mannai Investment Co Ltd v Eagle Star Assurance Co Ltd* (1995) where a lease commencing on 13 January and determinable on three months' notice expired on the third anniversary of its commencement. The tenant gave notice on 24 June to expire on 12 January 1995 (ie more than six months' notice). The landlord claimed this was incorrect notice.

It was held that the landlord was correct. For a lease starting on 1 January for one year, notice must be effective on 1 January and not on 31 December. Similarly, the last moment of 12 January is not the first moment of the 13 January.

Remedies by landlord for breach of covenant by tenant

1. Forfeiture

This is the main remedy. Remember this can only be used if there is an express clause in the lease allowing a right of re-entry.

Re-entry may be effected by:
- Peacefully re-entering
  Using force is a criminal act. If the property is a dwelling house, a landlord may only re-enter if he has a court order, otherwise he may be criminally liable under s 2 of the Protection from Eviction Act 1977. In effect, this also now applies to commercial premises unless the property is unoccupied. This was affirmed in *Billson v Residential Apartments Ltd* (1992) where the landlord entered business premises without a court order and it was held he had acted illegally.

  This means peaceable re-entry requires:
  (a) that the premises are not used as a residence; and
  (b) that there is nobody on the premises who tries to prevent entry.
  After re-entry the locks may be changed and a notice should be put up stating that the landlord has re-entered and that the tenant can no longer lawfully enter.
- By issuing a writ for possession
  The forfeiture takes effect from the date the writ is served (*Associated Deliveries Ltd v Harrison* (1985)).

Note
- If a landlord has condoned the breach he is deemed to have waived his right of forfeiture.

Acceptance of rent amounts to waiver. In *Central Estates (Belgravia) Ltd v Woolgas* (1972), a landlord took rent after the breach occurred, unaware that he would then loose his right of forfeiture. His action had waived the breach.

In *Van Haarlem v Kasner* (1992), a lease contained a covenant not to use the property for unlawful purposes. The tenant was charged with spying. The landlord considered forfeiture but continued to accept rent. Later when the tenant had been convicted he sought forfeiture. It was not given; he had waived his right to it.

Waiver cannot be avoided by a demand for, or an acceptance of, rent 'without prejudice' (*Expert Clothing Service & sales Ltd v Hillgate House Ltd* (1985)).

- Forfeiture notice must be correctly addressed
  In *Willow Green Ltd v Smithers* (1994), a lease of a flat contained a provision for forfeiture for breach of covenant to pay rent. D and his mother had never lived in the flat, but after some years, D's mother died, and D allowed his stepfather to move into the flat on the condition that he paid the rent and the service charge. His stepfather later disappeared owing several years' rent. The landlord sent a notice to the flat under s 146 of the LPA 1925 and later a summons for possession. D never received either the notice or the summons. The court found that possession should not be allowed. A place where a person is never present at all cannot be his address for the purposes of a summons. The word 'address' is to be construed as to its ordinary meaning. The Court of Appeal ruled that a summons for possession had never been properly served on a tenant when it had been posted to an address at which the tenant had never resided.

Forfeiture for breaches of covenant other than failure to pay rent

The landlord must serve a written notice in conformity with s 146(1) of the LPA 1925. Such notice must:

- specify the breach;
- require the breach be remedied if it is remediable;
- state any compensation required.

And if:

- the breach is a breach of a covenant to repair; and
- there are at least three more years of the lease to run and the original lease was for at least seven years; and
- it is not a lease of an agricultural tenancy,

then the landlord must advise the tenant of his rights under the Leasehold Property (Repairs) Act 1938 as amended by s 51 of the Landlord and Tenant Act (LATA) 1954.

The tenant may serve a counter-notice on the landlord within 28 days requiring him to obtain a court order for possession. If the landlord brings an action for possession, the tenant can ask for relief under s 146(2) of the LPA 1925 and the court will exercise its discretion in the matter.

Forfeiture for non-payment of rent

In this instance, the landlord makes a formal demand for rent between sunrise and sunset on the relevant day, unless there is a clause specifically excluding the necessity for such notice. If the rent is six months in arrears and distress would be inadequate, this necessity for a clause is waived under s 210 of the Common Law Procedure Act (CLPA) 1852.

The tenant has a statutory right to have the action stayed by paying the arrears and costs and the court can exercise its discretion in the matter.

Note

Forfeiture is not available for irremediable breaches.

In *Rugby School Governors v Tannalill* (1935) serious immorality (using house for prostitution) was an irremediable breach.

In *Glass v Kencakes* (1966), a tenant who evicted a sub-tenant immediately on learning she was using the house for prostitution was held not to have committed an irremediable breach; but see *Expert Clothing Service and Sales Ltd v Hillgate Home Ltd* (1986).

The test is can the covenant actually be remedied? In the *Expert Clothing Service* case, a positive covenant was not implemented. Clearly it could have been, so it was not irremediable, whereas a 'once for all' negative covenant is. This is why in *Kelly v Purvis* (1983) use as a brothel was deemed irremediable.

A s 146 notice must be served before re-entry.

Bhojwani v Kingsley Investment Ltd (1992) reasserted the view that a tenant may successfully apply for relief from forfeiture even if the landlord has sold the property in the meantime. This means that in this case he reasserted the traditional view which was made uncertain by *Fuller v Judy Properties Ltd* (1991).

2. Sue for damages for breach of covenant

3. An injunction to prevent the breach

4. Levy distress, but only for arrears of rent

The landlord must act in accordance with the CLPA 1852 and enter the premises without breaking down an outer door and do so between sunrise and sunset to distrain goods. These goods may then be sold to pay the arrears. No court action is required. This is true even if there is an interim order under the Insolvency Act 1986.

It was held in *McMullen & Sons Ltd v Cerrone* (1994) that leave of the court was not required even in such a situation.

Assignment of leases

A tenant may sell his lease to another person who becomes the new tenant. This is an assignment of the lease. A landlord may sell the property which is the subject of a lease to another, who then becomes the landlord. This is called assigning (selling) the reversion because when the lease is terminated the property will revert to the new landlord.

Section 19(1) of the LATA 1927 provides that a landlord cannot unreasonably withhold consent to a tenant's assigning his lease and the LATA 1988 states that in the case of all requests to assign by a tenant, made after 29 September 1988, where there are covenants, landlords must grant consent within a reasonable time or grant subject to conditions. If conditions are imposed or a refusal of consent is made, the landlord must be able to prove his refusal, or conditions he imposes are reasonable.

Reasonable means the grounds for refusal must not be made for personal reasons, eg appearance.

The Landlord and Tenant (Covenants) Act (LT(C)A) 1995 contains new provisions on assignment for leases made after 1 January 1996 (see below on enforceability of covenants). The LT(C)A 1995 introduces a new s 19(1A) to the LATA 1927, allowing landlords to prescribe before the lease is granted the conditions under which they will consent to an assignment. If later consent is refused on one of these, the landlord will not be regarded as withholding consent unreasonably. The conditions stated must conform with certain factual (eg ability to pay rent) or discretional grounds.

Leasehold covenants: enforceability

This has been modified by the LT(C)A 1995 which removes privity of contract between landlord and tenant from land law as regards covenants.

Covenants are contracts which place a burden on a covenantor or his land and give a benefit to the covenantee or his land. Whether the benefit or burden is on the person or the land depends on the substance of the covenant. Usually the covenantor (ie the one who takes the covenant) is the leaseholder and the covenantee (who observes the covenant) is the landlord.

Enforceability when the original parties to the covenant remain the same

For leases existing before 1 January 1996

Traditionally the original parties to the contract are always liable on the covenant because there is privity of contract between them, and this is true even if either assigned his or her interest and whatever the nature of the contract. It does not matter if the covenant was a personal one.

In the *City of London Corporation v Fell* (1992) and *Herbert Duncan Ltd v Cluttons* (1992), the original tenant had correctly assigned his lease but the new tenants (the assignees) had defaulted on the payment of rent so the landlord sued the original tenant.

The court held that in *Fell* the original tenant had obtained an extension of his lease on the assignment. It was a business tenancy so the extension was held to have created a new lease, and there was no liability on the covenant for the former tenant.

In *Cluttons*, there was no new tenancy so the original tenant was still liable.

Note

Leave was given in the case of *Fell* to appeal to the House of Lords on the grounds that where a lease is extended under the Landlord and Tenant Acts the original tenants should still be liable on leasehold covenants. The House of Lords decided that where an assignee has failed to pay rent, the business tenant is still liable until the tenancy ends on the due contract date.

Friends Provident Life Office v BR Board (1995)

In this case, it was held that a deed of variation of a lease made between a landlord's predecessor in title and the original tenant's successor in title who increased the rent did not affect the original tenant's continuing obligation to pay the original rent required under the original lease when a subsequent assignee defaulted.

For leases made after 31 December 1995

Section 5(1) of the new LT(C)A 1995 alters the position, and brings into effect the recommendations of the Law Commission's report of 1988. All leases after 31 December 1995 are to be classified as 'new' leases and landlords of such leases will not be able to sue ex-tenants on the basis of privity of contract. Such releases of tenants are automatic on the principle that landlords usually control any assignment of a lease by a tenant. It means that the original tenant is no longer liable on the whole term of the lease unless there is a clause making any assignment subject to the landlord's consent, ie the tenant comes within s 16 of the LT(C)A 1995 which allows the landlord, in certain circumstances, to require the tenant to enter into 'an authorised guarantee agreement' of the tenant's assignee's performance of the covenants while that assignee holds the lease. If that assignee, himself, assigns the lease, then the tenant who made the original assignment is released from such guarantee. The circumstances in which the landlord may require such 'authorised guarantee' are:

- where there is a covenant against assignment;
- where there is express provision in the lease that consent will only be given if the tenant signs an 'authorised guarantee';
- where the requirement is reasonable.

Note

These new provisions on assignments are only for new leases.

The LT(C)A 1995 does not release the landlord from breaches committed by his successors unless he has given the tenant notice that he wishes to be released from his obligations (see below).

Enforceability when the tenant changes but the landlord remains the same

In this case the tenant has assigned his lease to a new tenant.

Enforceability for leases made before 1 January 1996

For these leases covenants are only enforceable against the assignee of the lease if the following two conditions are satisfied:

- That the covenants 'have reference to the subject matter of the lease', ie if they are not personal covenants. This is sometimes expressed as the covenants 'touch and concern the land'. Some Examination Boards prefer 'touch and concern the land' used only for freehold covenants. If a covenant does not satisfy this criterion it 'does not run with the land'.

  Swift Investments v Combined English Stores (1988) set a three-pronged test for this requirement:

  (a) is it worded so as to be personal? (no);

  (b) is the nature or quality of the land affected by it? (yes);

(c) is the original covenantee (landlord) the only estate owner to benefit from it? (yes).

Note

Difficulties have arisen where a covenant involves the payment of money, but such a covenant has been deemed to 'have reference to the subject matter of a lease' where it involved a surety to pay money for a breach, as in the *Swift Investments* case.

- That there is privity of estate between the original landlord and the assignee (ie the new tenant).
  Spencer's case is authority that there is such privity so that the burden of the covenant 'runs with the land' and the assignee is bound by the original covenant.

Enforceability for leases made after 31 December 1995, ie under the LT(C)A 1995

- For these covenants there is no requirement that they should 'have reference to the subject matter of the lease', ie 'touch and concern the land'. The LT(C)A 1995 abolishes such a requirement. All covenants made after this date (personal or not) will be deemed to have passed the burden and benefit on assignment unless they are expressed to be personal. This is the effect of s 3 of the LT(C)A 1995.
- The requirement of privity is unaltered.

Note

If the assignee is in breach of covenant, the landlord can only sue the original tenant if there has been an authorised agreement to that effect (see above).

Enforceability of leasehold covenants where an assignee of the original or subsequent tenant assigns his lease, ie where there has been more than one assignment of the lease

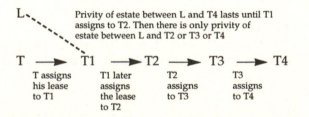

L

Privity of estate between L and T4 lasts until T1 assigns to T2. Then there is only privity of estate between L and T2 or T3 or T4

T ⟶ T1 ⟶ T2 ⟶ T3 ⟶ T4

T assigns his lease to T1

T1 later assigns the lease to T2

T2 assigns to T3

T3 assigns to T4

(a) Enforceability for leases made before 1 January 1996

Where there has been more than one assignment of the original lease, ie where there has been a succession of tenants, *Spencer's* case still applies so that T4, the present tenant, may be sued by L, the original landlord because there is privity of estate between them providing the covenant 'has reference to the subject matter of the lease'.

Problem 1

Section 79 of the LPA 1925 implies that a tenant will be bound by the covenants providing there is no express provision to the contrary in the lease. T4, the present tenant, has no money.

What can L do?

L can sue the original tenant T because there is still privity of contract between L and T.

Problem 2

What can T then do ?

T can do one of the following:

- Use s 77 of the LPA 1925. This section implies a covenant by the assignee to indemnify the tenant who assigned the lease to him for any breach of covenant he may make. This means that:
  (a)   T can sue T1 under the indemnity;
  (b)   T1 can sue T2;
  (c)   T2 can sue T3;
  (d)   T3 can sue T4.

  There is a difficulty, however, if one tenant has disappeared.
- Use the rule in *Moule v Garrett* (1872) that where debts are joint and only one is sued, the others have an obligation to pay.

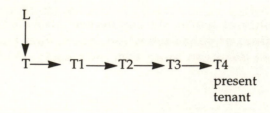

Example

L may sue T or T4 for breach of covenant.

Under the rule in *Moule v Garrett*, if L sues T, T can sue T4. However, this may be pointless because L may be suing T because T4 has no money.

Note

L cannot sue T1, T2 or T3 because there is no longer any privity of estate between them.

The following case illustrates that an assignee should be careful not to commit himself inadvertently to carry out the covenants for the full term of the lease even when he has assigned it.

Estates Gazette Ltd v Benjamin Restaurants (1995)
The original lessee of some premises assigned it to a new lessee who agreed to fulfil the covenants in the original lease; a surety covenanted with the landlord that this would be done. There were then subsequent assignments of the lease and one of these assignees then defaulted on the covenant to pay rent. The plaintiff then claimed the rent from the first assignee and his surety. This first assignee claimed he was not liable because he was not the original tenant and had assigned to another.

It was held that he had agreed by the words used that he would be responsible for the covenants during the whole of the lease.

Enforceability for leases made after 31 December 1995

Assignees of the original tenants of new leases which fall within the LT(C)A 1995 will automatically be released form any future liabilities for breach of covenant when they assign the lease, ie the covenants are not enforceable against them. This means the assignee is in the same position as the original tenant should he assign his lease, the landlord can only sue the present tenant T4, the one to whom the last assignment was made.

Again there is no requirement of the covenant's 'having reference to the subject matter of the lease'.

Enforceability when the landlord changes

Enforceability of leasehold covenants where the original landlord assigns his reversion of the lease

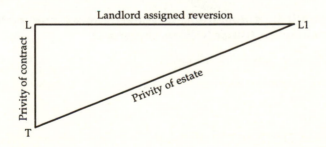

Enforceability for leases made before 1 January 1996

In this situation the tenant remains the same and the landlord changes so that:

- There is still privity of contract between the original tenant and the original landlord so that L can still sue T for breach of contract.
- There is now privity of estate between the original tenant and his new landlord L1. Sections 141 and 142 of the LPA 1925 have been construed to mean that the benefits and burdens of the covenants will run provided they have 'reference to the subject matter of the lease', unless there are specific clauses to the contrary. Section 141 serves to pass the benefit and s 142 to pass the burden. This means that L1 can sue T for breach of covenant.

Caerns Motor Services Ltd v Texaco Ltd (1995)

Lessees of Texaco covenanted to buy petrol only from Texaco, their landlord. Texaco then assigned their reversion. It was held that the benefit and burden of the solus agreement ran to the assignee of the lease because the covenant had reference to the subject matter of the lease and was, therefore, within ss 141 and 142.

Enforceability for leases made after 31 December 1995

- Under the LT(C)A 1995, ss 141 and 142 of the LPA 1925 are repealed and there is no longer privity of contract between landlord and tenant so that L can no longer sue T for breach of contract.
- There is privity of estate between L1 and T so that L1 can sue T in the same way as before the LT(C)A 1995 except that there is no requirement that the covenants 'have reference to the subject matter of the lease'.

Note

L, the original landlord, is not automatically released from his obligations towards his ex-tenant, T, on the assignment of his reversion. He must apply for release (see p 80 above).

Enforceability of leasehold covenants when the assignee of the reversion himself then assigns it

This is where a new landlord assigns his reversion to a further landlord.

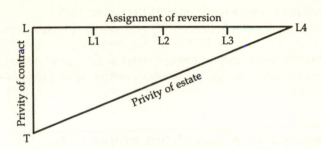

Enforceability for leases made before 1 January 1996

- L can sue T on the original contract because there is privity of contract between them.
- Providing the covenants 'have reference to the subject matter of the lease', L4 can sue T because there is privity of estate between them. There is no privity of estate between L1 and T;

L2 and T;

L3 and T.

Problem

Can L4 sue T for breaches committed while L1, L2 or L3 was T's landlord?

Answer

In the past: Yes. Sections 141 and 142 of the LPA 1925 have been deemed not to require privity of estate as illustrated by *London and County (A & D) Ltd v Wilfred Sportsman Ltd* (1971) which concerned a lease, for 21 years, of two properties with a covenant for payment of rent and a proviso for re-entry for breach. Before the expiry of the 21 years, the original landlord had assigned the reversion. The new landlord found out that the tenants had not paid the rent under the previous landlord; there were arrears when the reversion was assigned to him.

It was held that s 141 allowed an assignee of the reversion to sue and re-enter for the arrears of rent payable before the assignment.

This is no longer possible under the LT(C)A 1995 because this Act stipulates that for all leases made before 31 December 1995, action to recover money (rent) from a former tenant can only be undertaken if that tenant has been served with notice by 1 July 1996.

Enforceability for leases made after 31 December 1995

L, the original landlord can no longer sue T, the original tenant, because s 141 of the LPA 1925 has been repealed under the LT(C)A 1995. A landlord also cannot bring an action for arrears of rent from a former tenant unless he has given notice within six months of the rent becoming due.

Sub-tenants and leasehold covenants

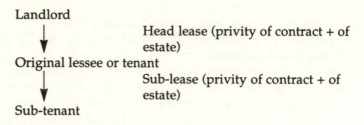

Landlord

Head lease (privity of contract + of estate)

Original lessee or tenant

Sub-lease (privity of contract + of estate)

Sub-tenant

- Between the landlord and the original tenant there is both privity of contract and privity of estate.
- Between the sub-tenant and the original tenant there is both privity of contract and of estate.
- Between the landlord and the sub-tenant there is neither privity or contact nor privity of estate.

This means that at common law that:

- The landlord cannot enforce any covenant that has reference to the subject matter of the lease against the sub-tenant.
- The sub-tenant cannot enforce any covenant having reference to the subject matter of the lease against the landlord.

But

If the sub-tenant breaches a covenant, the tenant is still liable to the landlord of the head lease, so that, if a tenant forfeits a lease, eg for breach of the covenant to pay rent, then the sub-tenant's lease is also determined.

The only recourse the sub-tenant then has is to use s 146 of the LPA 1925 and apply to the courts for relief.

The landlord may be able to proceed against the sub-tenant in equity under the rule in *Tulk v Moxhay* (1848) provided the following conditions are satisfied that:

- the covenant is negative in substance;
- the covenant has reference to the subject matter of the lease, unless made after 1 January 1996;

- there is no contrary clause in the sub-lease;
- the sub-tenant had actual, implied or constructive notice of the covenant.

The sub-lease will not become forfeit but damages may be awarded or an injunction granted to prevent further breaches.

Hemingway Securities Ltd v Dunraven Ltd (1995). The tenants had broken a restrictive covenant on sub-letting. The sub-tenants were bound by the covenant under *Tulk v Moxhay*.

Implied covenants

The following covenants are 'usual' covenants expressed or implied in leases.

The landlord's covenants are:
- to allow quiet enjoyment (ie not to harass or disturb) and not to derogate from his grant. Any harassment of a tenant by a landlord is a criminal offence under the Protection from Eviction Act 1977.

The tenant's covenants are:

- to pay rent;
- not to assign or sub-let without the landlord's consent;
- to keep in repair.

Note
Section 19(1) of the LATA 1927, which means that even if a lease contains an express clause against assignment the lease must state the landlord shall not refuse consent to assignment except on reasonable grounds.

The LATA 1988 requires a landlord to consider a written request for consent from a tenant and give either written consent (with any restrictions) or refuse consent in writing giving reasons.

In *Air India v Balabel* (1993), there was a lease for 20 years with a covenant not to assign without the landlord's consent and such consent was not to be unreasonably withheld. The tenant applied for consent. The landlord refused giving written reasons. The tenant still assigned his lease. The landlord began proceedings for forfeiture and the tenant argued that the reasons for the refusal of consent to assignment were unreasonable.

The landlord's action was upheld. The landlord had given, as reasons, the fact that the proposed assignee had failed to pay rent for premises which his company occupied elsewhere; and that the business he proposed to run in the premises to which consent was refused had also failed elsewhere. In addition, the proposed assignee had a precarious financial history.

The court held that the landlord was entitled to consider such matters. They were conclusions that might be reached by a reasonable man in the circumstances, as required in *Pimms Ltd v Tallow Chandlers Co* (1964).

Remember a legal assignment must be by deed (*Crago v Julian* (1992)).

For the present position, see the LT(C)A 1995 on p 78 above.

The Leasehold Reform Act 1967

This enables a tenant who has occupied his residence for at least five years (or periods equivalent to five years in the last 10 years) under a lease *originally* granted for a term exceeding 21 years at a low rent, to acquire the freehold of that residence or to obtain an extension of his lease for 50 years after the present lease expires.

Note
This relates to houses only, not to flats in a horizontally divided building.

The Leasehold Reform Housing and Urban Development Act 1993

This came into force on 1 November 1993. It gives new rights to many leaseholders including those in flats. Included is:

* an option of extending a lease for 90 years or more;
* an option of combining with other flat holders to buy the freehold jointly; provided the original lease was for 21 years. The clauses and procedures are outside the scope of this book.

Commonholds

One of the problems of freehold flats ('flying freeholds') has been creating suitable arrangements for the upkeep of the whole building of which a flat is a part, and the maintenance of the common areas such as stairways, lifts, entrances. Leaseholders normally pay a service charge for this.

It has been suggested that a new form of estate, a commonhold, should be created, so that a freehold flat-holder of say, a top floor flat, should not be left with the whole burden of a new roof should the roof be blown off in a gale; or a second floor flat-owner be faced with a bill for damage to his flat because a third floor flat above has fallen in for lack of maintenance. It is envisaged that all the freehold flat-owners (owners and leaseholders) should form a commonhold association to take care of such matters, and that they should be legally bound to contribute to the upkeep of the common areas and overall structure.

Question hints

Questions on leases usually fall under the following heads:

Lease v licence
This is considered at the end of Chapter 7.

Covenants in leases
Questions on covenants in leases are almost invariably of the problem type involving assignments of the lease and of the reversion, and remedies for breach of covenant. It is often helpful to draw a simple diagram if there are a number of assignments and sub-leases. Put the date by each.

Consider each assignment, noting whether there is privity of estate, privity of contract, or neither for leases made before 1 January 1996. This will tell you whom you can sue. Remember the differences for leases made under the LATA 1995 for leases made since then.

Note the covenants which have been broken. What are the remedies and who can exert them? Remember forfeiture is not available unless there is a specific clause to that effect in the lease, and that the covenant to pay rent does not need a s 146 notice, but, that if it is a covenant to repair, you may have to refer to s 51 of the LATA 1954.

Are the covenants remediable?

Note
Expert Clothing Service v Hillgate Home (1986).

Make sure the s 146 notice, or a writ for possession, are served correctly (*Billson v Residential Apartments* and *Willow Green Ltd v Smithers*).

Have the lessees protected themselves against breaches committed by their successors in title? Have they assigned properly? (*Crago v Julian*). Did the landlord consent? Again, remember the differences for leases made after 1 January 1996.

If there is a sub-lease remember the landlord may be able to act against the sub-tenant under *Tulk v Moxhay* but only if the covenant is negative in substance.

Finally consider an application by the lessee or by the sub-tenant for relief.

Questions on legal and equitable leases

You will need to consider how the lease was made, eg was it made by deed? If not, you will need to pay attention to the length of the lease, whether any rent has been paid and whether s 40 of the LPA 1925 or s 2 of the Law of Property (MIscellaneous Provisions) Act 1989 applies. Problems of this kind may be framed so that you have to consider whether you are dealing with a lease or a licence (Chapter 7).

7 Licences

You should be familiar with the following areas:

- types
- revocation
- contractual licences and third parties
- proprietary estoppel

Types

There are four types of licence: bare licences; licences coupled with a grant or interest; contractual licences; and licences protected by estoppel.

Bare licences

A bare licence is mere permission. Such permission can be revoked by notice, so that the licensee becomes a trespasser. No valuable consideration has been given by the licensee.

Licences coupled with a grant or interest

These are licences necessary to enter land to avail oneself of an interest, eg a profit *à prendre*. The licence is an implied one and lasts as long as the interest lasts. Such licences are binding on third parties.

Contractual licences

These require:

- offer;
- acceptance;

- valuable consideration;
- an intention to create legal relations.

It is often very difficult to decide whether there was an intention to create a legal relationship when the arrangement was an informal one (*Errington v Errington and Woods* (1952)). The courts will consider all the circumstances to impute a common intention by both parties.

The following case illustrates this. In *Tanner v Tanner* (1965), a mistress and her children lived in accommodation which was a protected tenancy. The man purchased a house for them to live in. The man and his mistress later quarrelled and the man claimed possession of the house.

The court held that the mistress had provided valuable consideration by giving up her protected tenancy. She had obtained a contractual licence which could not be revoked until the children had left school.

In *Horrocks v Foray* (1976), a man installed his mistress and her child in a house he had bought. He died, and left his whole estate to his wife. The wife claimed possession.

It was held that the man's executives could obtain possession, the mistress had provided no valuable consideration so she had not obtained a contractual licence. There had been no intention to create legal relations.

In *Coombes v Smith* (1986), a married women left her husband to live with a man by whom she had had a child.

The court held that there was no contractual licence. There was no intention to create a legal relationship and the woman had given no valuable consideration.

In *Chandler v Kerley* (1978), Mr and Mrs K and their children lived in a house on which Mr K paid the mortgage instalments. They quarrelled and Mr K left, but still paid the mortgage. Mrs K met C and they became lovers. Then Mr K was unable to keep up the mortgage payment, so Mr and Mrs K agreed to sell the house. They found this difficult, so Mr Chandler bought it at a greatly reduced price, on the understanding that he, Mrs K and the children would live there together.

Six weeks later Mrs K and C quarrelled and C gave Mrs K notice to quit (but it was clear he had not bought the house with this intention).

The court found that Mrs K had a contractual licence but not for life. The agreement was intended to be binding, but it must not be inferred that C had intended to look after Mrs K's children for ever. The relationship between Mrs K and C had clearly ended, so the contractual licence could be ended by reasonable notice, and 12 months was reasonable.

The revocation of a contractual licence

The position at common law

The licensor may revoke the licence at any time and if this leads to a breach of contract the licensee is entitled to damages only.

In *Wood v Leadbitter* (1845), a man bought a ticket for a race course. He created a disturbance and was ejected. He brought an action for assault.

It was held that his admission ticket gave him a licence to be in the ground and nothing more, so that once that licence was revoked he became a trespasser. The licensor was entitled to use reasonable force to remove him. He could not sue for assault, only for breach of contract for which there would be only nominal damages.

The position after the Judicature Acts 1873–75

The Judicature Acts 1873–75 brought equity into the matter.

Hurst v Picture Theatres Ltd (1915) established that where there is an agreement not to revoke a licence which has been given, and this agreement has been accompanied by valuable consideration, it is a breach of contract to breach the agreement not to revoke.

In this case, a person who had bought a cinema ticket was ejected before he had seen all of the film. The court held he was entitled to be ejected in law (as in *Wood v Leadbitter*) but not in equity, because the contract was a specifically enforceable one. This meant he was no longer a trespasser.

In *Winter Garden Theatre (London) Ltd v Millennium Productions Ltd* (1948), the House of Lords held that whether or not a contractual licence is revocable depended on the actual agreement.

In *Hounslow London Borough Council v Twickenham Garden Developments Ltd* (1971) the defendant company made a contract that they would prepare a site for development. The plaintiffs thought they were being too slow and ended the contract. D refused to accept the termination and continued to work on the site so P applied for an injunction to prevent D from entering the site.

D entered the site under a licence implied in the contract.

The court considered *Hurst* and *Winter Garden Theatre* and Megarry VC held that the court would not aid P by granting an injunction to prevent D entering the site, because it would be inequitable to do so. What P was really after was to make D in a breach of contract. It is irrelevant if the licence to enter land was not the main purpose of the contract.

Note

Where the contractual licence is the only agreement the court will grant specific performance.

In *Verrall v Great Yarmouth Borough Council* (1981), the council granted the National Front permission to use a hall for a meeting. After local council elections the new council purported to revoke the licence.

The court held that specific performance would be granted. A licence supported by valuable consideration cannot be revoked.

Contractual licences and third parties

There are two conflicting views: the traditional and the more recent.

The traditional view

In this view, a contractual licence cannot give a proprietary interest in land, ie a right in the land itself, so that it cannot bind a third party, whether that third party had notice of it or not.

A licence is a purely personal agreement so that it is only enforceable by the parties to the contract. This means that if the land is sold the purchaser is not bound by the licence.

In *King v David Allen and Sons, Billposting Ltd* (1916), D had a contract to put up posters on the wall of a cinema. This was a licence for a fixed period. The cinema was then sold.

It was held that the new owners were not bound by the licence. The only thing D could do was to sue P for breach of contract.

The more modern view

This is based on Lord Denning's use of equity to make a licence binding on third parties.

In *Errington v Errington and Woods* (1952), a father bought a house (by deposit and mortgage) for his married son and his wife to live in. He agreed to transfer the house to them if they lived in it and paid all the mortgage instalments. They kept the building society book and paid the instalments. The father died, and the son and his wife split up; the wife stayed in the house and continued to pay the mortgage. The son went back to his mother. His mother then claimed possession of the house.

The court decided that contract had been met; they had lived there and paid the mortgage. As a result, the contractual licence could not be revoked and since the son's wife paid the mortgage she could not be evicted. They had not been tenants-at-will, because, if this had been the case, the father could have evicted them at any time and he could not; he could only do so if the terms of the licence had been breached (this is a view contrary to *Wood v Leadbitter*).

Lord Denning developed his use of equity in cases of contractual licence to give a proprietary interest in land under a constructive trust.

In *Binions v Evans* (1972), Evans, an employee of the Tredegar Estate was living in a rent-free cottage. When he died the trustees of the estate allowed his widow to continue living there as a 'tenant-at-will', free of the rent for the rest of her life on condition she looked after it. The terms were part of an express agreement.

The trustees sold the cottage at a low price because of her tenancy and the agreement, of which the purchaser had full knowledge. Six months later Mrs Evans was given notice to quit.

The court refused to give the purchaser a possession order, but the judges were divided on their reasons for this decision.

Lord Denning dissenting, found Mrs Evans had neither a legal estate nor a legal interest in the land; she was not a tenant but did have a contractual licence which had been revocable, but when the purchaser bought the cottage with notice of that licence, equity imposed an constructive trust and the purchaser held the cottage on trust for her until she died. Lord Denning emphasised that where a licensee is in actual occupation, any purchaser with notice of this is bound by that licence. He reaffirmed his stance in *Errington v Errington and Woods*.

The majority view held there was no tenancy-at-will which could be revoked. What Mrs Evans really had was an equitable life interest under s 20(1)(iv) of the Settled Land Act (SLA) 1925; she was a tenant for years determinable on life, not holding merely under a lease at a rent. Such an interest could be overreached but had not been in this instance because the purchaser had had notice of it.

On this basis there was no need to consider the two options:

- whether the agreement gave rise to a contractual licence to occupy which was irrevocable; or
- whether a contractual licence gave rise to an estate or interest in land as in *Errington*.

Other cases where a contractual licence has been held to give rise to a constructive trust

There are other cases where a contractual licence has given rise to a right against third parties, ie where occupation under such a licence has given a *proprietary interest in land* without conformity with s 52(1) and s 53(1)(a)(b) of the Law of Property Act (LPA) 1925. Examples of such cases are as follows:

In *Ungarian v Lesnoff* (1989), a man met his mistress (D) in Poland. She moved to England with him and took British nationality. He bought a house with title in his name only. D lived in the house with him and her two grown-up sons and a son of P. D and her sons made improvements to the house. D and P quarrelled; P left and claimed the house.

The court held that the circumstances were such that an intention could be inferred that D would be able to live there for the rest of her life (*cf Binions v Evans*). P, therefore, held the house on trust for her, ie the court created settled land within SLA 1925 (following the majority view in *Binions v Evans*).

Problem
If land is settled land, why cannot the tenant for life sell it?

In *Re Sharpe (A Bankrupt)* (1980), a nephew borrowed £12,000 from his aunt to buy property priced at £17,000. The aunt was to live with her nephew and his wife in it. She was not in good health, and they were to look after her. The nephew became bankrupt and the trustee-in-bankruptcy sought vacant possession of the house.

The aunt claimed either:

• a beneficial interest in the house; or
• a contractual licence to occupy it.

It was held that she had a contractual licence which was not revocable until the loan was repaid, and which arose, therefore, under a constructive trust resulting in an interest binding the trustee-in-bankruptcy or any third party.

A return to tradition?

The traditional view was re-affirmed in *Ashburn Anstalt v Arnold* (1989) by the Court of Appeal. Here it was stated that licences do not give interests in land; they only give personal rights which could be revoked. They cannot bind third parties.

In *Ashburn Anstalt*, the contractual licence was held to be under a constructive trust and so binding on a purchaser where, because of the purchaser's actions, it would have been inequitable for there to be no contractual licence. This is not, however, giving the licensee an interest in the land itself. The constructive trust so found by the court is for the particular purchaser personally.

Licences protected by estoppel

These are licences which give rise to a proprietary interest in land because the licensee has spent money on some improvement to property, and where there cannot be a constructive trust because there was never any common intention that such an interest should be acquired. (In the case of constructive trusts and contractual licences, such common intention was imputed by the circumstances under which the licensee occupied the property.)

You should be aware, however, that many of the cases involving a contractual licence could possibly have come within proprietary estoppel.

Proprietary estoppel

A proprietary interest in land may be acquired in equity under proprietary estoppel without the need for a deed or writing in accordance with ss 52 and 53 of the LPA 1925.

Proprietary estoppel requires:

• an expenditure on the property, ie an act to one's detriment;
• that such expenditure was made in the mistaken belief, by the person making it, that he or she did have an interest in the property;
• that the title holder of the property knew that such expenditure was being made, and that it was being made, in the mistaken belief of the person making it, that he did have an interest in the property;
• equity to intervene and estop the legal title holder from denying that the person making such expenditure had an interest in the property.

The principle was established in *Ramsden v Dyson* (1866) and affirmed recently in *Taylor Fashions Ltd v Liverpool Victoria Trustee Co Ltd* (1981) but in *Taylor Fashions* it was stressed that the emphasis is now on the actions of the persons claiming proprietary estoppel rather than on the title holder of the property. That the 'title holder knew' the person was acting to his detriment in the mistaken belief that he had an interest in the property means that he had actual, implied, or constructive knowledge, so that it would inequitable to allow such title holder to exert his strict legal rights.

The following cases illustrate proprietary estoppel.

In *Dillwyn v Llewellyn* (1862) a father gave his son land but did not make a conveyance by deed, only by a memorandum. The son, in the belief he held the land, built a house on it. When his father died, the land was claimed as part of the father's estate.

The court held that although 'equity will not assist a volunteer', the executors were estopped from denying the imperfect gift; it would be unconscionable not to vest the fee simple in the son.

In *Inwards v Baker* (1965), the son built a bungalow on his father's land; father and son paying for its erection in almost equal amounts, but the son did the actual building. The father had suggested the bungalow was built there. The son lived in the bungalow and believed he would be able to do so for as long as he wished, if need be for life; but when the father died he left the land to someone else.

It was held that the son had acted to his detriment in the mistaken belief he could always live in the bungalow; his father had known this. The son would be allowed to live there as long as he pleased even if the title to the land changed hands but the land would not be vested in the son.

In *Pascoe v Turner* (1979), P bought a house in which he lived with his mistress. He told her both the house and its contents were hers (although he held the legal title). In reliance on this belief, she spent her own money on improvements, repairs and furniture. When the relationship ended he gave her notice to quit.

She was held to be a licensee but had acted in reliance on his promise, so that he was estopped from evicting her; she had acted to her detriment. In this case, the court not only allowed her to remain in occupation; it actually ordered the legal estate to be conveyed to her (this means his imperfect gift would be perfected in equity).

In *Greasely v Cooke* (1980), D was a servant in a widower's house. She looked after the widower, his sons and a mentally ill daughter. She also had a relationship with one of the sons. She was told that when the widower died she could live in the house for as long as she wished, but she received no payment for her services. Then the brothers to whom the house had been left tried to evict her.

They were estopped from doing so. She had acted to her detriment in reliance she could remain there, and the onus was on the legal title holders to rebut this; they could not do so.

In *Crabb v Arun DC* (1976), a person, D, owned two plots of land but only one had access to a road (Plot X). When he sold the plots he assured the buyer of Plot X orally, that access to it would be granted. When he sold the other plot he did not reserve this right of access to Plot X. The new owner refused such access.

D was estopped from reneging on his word. The owner of Plot X had acquired an easement of access.

Griffiths v Williams (1977) involved an informal, family agreement. Mrs G had a married daughter, Mrs W, who lived in a house owned by Mrs Cole (Mrs G's mother, Mrs W's grandmother). Mrs C had told her granddaughter that the house would be hers when she died, so Mrs W spend a considerable sum of her own money on repairs and improvements to it. When Mrs C died, a later will was discovered leaving the house not to Mrs W, but to her mother, Mrs G.

The court declared that estoppel applied. Mrs W had acted to her detriment in the mistaken belief the house would be hers and Mrs C had allowed this, knowing the belief was mistaken. Mrs W was given a lease determinable on death at a nominal rent; she would not be given a life interest since this would make it settled land and give her a power to sell or assign.

In *ER Ives Investment Ltd v High* (1967), the foundations of a block of flats mistakenly encroached on adjacent land. The neighbour having objected, was compensated by being given a right of way across the surroundings of the flats so that he could reach a garage he then built, from the road.

Was this a licence or an easement?

When the block of flats was sold, there was a clause that sale was subject to the neighbour's right of way, but the neighbour had not registered this right as a Class D(iii) land charge, ie as an equitable easement (the land was unregistered). The new owners argued the right was a licence and, even if it were an easement, was not binding on them because it was not registered.

The court held that the right was binding. The access way could be seen, so they did have notice of it and were estopped from denying use of it.

In any case, the foundations had imposed a burden on neighbouring land so the owner of that land was entitled to claim a benefit. This was a fundamental rule of law.

This raises a further problem.

What if the land had been registered? There is doubt as to whether the right is really a licence by estoppel, or an equitable easement; if it is the latter it is doubtful whether it would have come within s 70(1)(a) of the Land Registration Act (LRA) 1925 as an overriding interest.

In *Re Basham* (1986), a mother remarried and her 16 year old daughter lived with her mother and stepfather. The daughter helped both in the house and in her stepfather's business and continued to do this after her mother had died. She moved away when she married, but when her stepfather became old and ill, she moved to be near him. She arranged for the house to have central heating and her husband did repairs and looked after the garden in her stepfather's house. Her stepfather repeated his promise to leave her the house and also said he would leave her son some money; but he died intestate.

It was held that she was entitled to the *entire* estate (this means she gained a property right by estoppel. But this right could only be exercised in the future, ie when he died).

This case must be considered in the light of the following:

- the estate was small in value;
- he had no close relatives and those entitled did not dispute her right to the house; the executors merely sought clarification of the position at law;
- the judge was not used to such cases and some have argued he confused proprietary and promissory estoppel;
- it is first instance only and there is much doubt about the decision. (It does, however, appear in the guise of an examination problem.)

Re Basham raises certain problems

What would have happened if he had left a will giving the cottage to someone else or to charity, or if he had sold the cottage had been living in it as a tenant paying rent?

In *Lim Teng Huan v Ang Swee Chan* (1992), P and D purchased land jointly but the conveyance was in the names of their respective fathers. Then P agreed to transfer his land to D in exchange for other land. This was done by a written agreement. D began to develop the land he had received from P. Then both fathers died. P claimed a half of the land P and D had purchased jointly.

It was held that the written agreement was not a deed that was unenforceable. The doctrine of proprietary estoppel applied and in equity P was ordered to convey his half-share of the land to D, and D was to pay appropriate compensation. D had relied to his detriment on P's assurance.

Note
This is a Privy Council case only but it illustrates the application of the principles in *Taylor Fashions Ltd v Liverpool Victoria Trustees* and shows how proprietary estoppel can be used to give specific performance to an unenforceable contract.

In *Matharu v Matharu* (1994), a wife was given a licence to occupy a house for the rest of her life under the doctrine of proprietary estoppel because, although the house belonged to her father-in-law, he had encouraged her to believe it belonged to her husband. In this belief her husband had carried out expensive repairs to it at his own expense. Her husband had paid the mortgage. After the marriage had broken down, thinking that the house was her husband's, she had put in a new kitchen.

It was held by a majority that proprietary estoppel gave her a licence to remain in the house provided she paid the outgoings, including the mortgage.

The dissenting view was that since all judges agreed there had been no common intention that she had an interest in the house, how could it be argued that she had a claim under estoppel?

Note: She was given a licence, not an interest, and a licence can be overridden if the property is sold.

Lord Justice Roch took the opportunity to re-emphasise the requirements of such estoppel as:

- The person relying on the doctrine had made a mistake as to his or her legal rights.
- That he or she had expended some money or done some act on the faith of that mistaken belief.
- That the possessor of the legal right knew of the existence of his or her legal right which if it existed was inconsistent with equity.
- That the possessor of the legal right knew of the other person's mistaken belief.
- That the possessor of the legal right had encouraged the other person in the expenditure of money or doing other acts on which that person relied.

Having found the existence of an equity of proprietary estoppel, the extent of the equity must then be determined.

In *Wayling v Jones* (1993), a couple cohabited for four years. P left. A year later at D's request, P returned to live with D. D then bought a cafe with living accommodation attached and promised to leave the property to P in his will. P was only paid pocket money for helping in the cafe. Subsequently, D sold the property and the couple moved several times. P acted as chauffeur and companion and helped in the business enterprises. Then D bought a hotel in Wales. Later, when D died, it was discovered that he had not updated his will and P received only the car and some furniture. P pleaded proprietary estoppel.

It was held that there was proprietary estoppel: there had been the necessary reliance and acts on that reliance and D had known this.

In *Sledmore v Dalby* (1996), a married couple, H and W, bought a house and allowed their daughter and her husband to live in it. H later conveyed his interest in the house to W and in the same year W made a will leaving the house to H and W's daughter. Shortly after H died and four years later the daughter died. W then sought possession of the house inhabited by her daughter's widower.

The Court of Appeal held that the widower based his claim for the right to remain in the house on estoppel because he had made some improvements to the house. The court held that these improvements were not sufficient to support estoppel and he had enjoyed rent-free accommodation for them. His parents-in-law had not conducted themselves in such a way that he was encouraged to do any acts to his detriment nor acquiesced in his so acting. He could only point to an assurance that W was leaving the house to her daughter. W now wished to move into a smaller house than the one she presently inhabited for which she could no longer afford the mortgage repayments. There was no proprietary estoppel.

Question hints

Essay questions

These usually fall into one of two groups:

- The lease/licence debate
  Here you will need to define the requirements of a lease as distinct from a licence, but your answer will centre on *Street v Mountford* and subsequent cases. Do not merely cite cases; use each to illustrate a different point, and to indicate the way case law is refining exclusive possession.
- Focusing on aspects of licences and proprietary interests in land
  You will need to point out how proprietary rights, ie interests in land are legally acquired. This means you will need to consider ss 52 and 53 of the LPA 1925 and to distinguish between the

different kinds of licences (remember a licence is permission only) and how these have been construed to give a proprietary rights. Attention must be paid to the revocation of contractual licences, and to case law where contractual licences and estoppel have given rights in land, and how such rights may or may not be protected.

You should indicate that there seems to be a return to the traditional view that a contractual licence will not be binding on third parties as indicated by the Court of Appeal in *Ashburn Anstalt v Arnold* (1989) where a contractual licence was held not to give (*obiter*) an overriding interest within s 70(1)(g) of the LRA 1925 and the court indicated the law as it stood before *Errington v Errington and Woods* (1952) was to be preferred (although on the facts *Errington* was correctly decided).

You should also consider the problem of *ER Investments v High*; the difficulties raised by such cases as *Binions v Evans* (the majority view) and settled land, and how the court avoids the problem in *Inwards v Baker* and *Griffith v Williams* and indicate the concern with which the Law Commission viewed such cases in Trusts of Land No 181 (1989) (see Chapter 3).

An essay question of this type will need careful planning and selection of material, and succinct expression if it is not to become rambling and too long.

Problem type questions

Again there are two basic types:

- Lease v Licence: you may be asked either to advise the landlord or to advise the tenant.

  In each case, you must emphasise that if there is a lease the tenant may be protected under the Rents Act 1977 or the Housing Act 1988, and that this is why you are structuring your answer to establish a lease rather than a licence or *vice versa*. Consider case law from *Street v Mountford*, but in each case relate to the facts of your problem to establish (or not) analogies. You will usually find some facts fit a given case, others do not. Indicate this, and then make a judgment on what you think the court will do, giving your reasons. Do not merely write out the facts of the case.

- Where the problem is clearly requiring consideration of licences rather than leases.

Again indicate that licences, as such, do not give proprietary interests in land. Make sure you know how the licence was acquired and when. (Was permission ever retracted? Is there a possibility of adverse possession? Examiners sometimes complicate the question this way but do not look for this if is clearly not there.) What sort of licence is it? Is there valuable consideration raising the possibility of a contractual licence? (Remember valuable means money or money's worth.) Is there action to his or her detriment by someone in the mistaken belief he or she was to have an interest in land? Did the landowner know this? If he did, look for proprietary estoppel. If there is an interest in land, has it been protected? If so, has it been correctly protected? Do not forget to see if the person you are advising needs a remedy: injunction? damages?

8 Freehold covenants

You should be familiar with the following areas:

- original parties
- assignments: benefits and burdens
- protection
- modification and discharge
- the Law Commission's proposals

Definition

A freehold covenant is a covenant made between owners of freehold land, imposing a burden on the land of the covenantor, and giving a benefit to the land of the covenantee. A covenant is a promise made by deed. The person making the promise is called the covenantor and the person who takes the promise from him is the covenantee. The original parties to the covenant, ie the original covenantee and original covenantor, are always liable on the covenant as parties to a contract. (Note there has been no change for freehold covenants as there has been for leasehold covenants – see Chapter 6.)

A covenant may be positive or negative. This is decided by its substance not its form, in other words, not by the way in which it is expressed. A positive covenant requires some action usually involving the covenantor in money.

Be careful
Positive covenants are often expressed in a negative form.

A covenant to keep a building in good repair is a positive covenant. It is positive in both substance and form.

A covenant not to allow a building to fall into disrepair is also a positive covenant. It is positive in substance though negative in form. The general rule is that positive covenants are usually only enforceable between the original parties to the covenant.

This was illustrated in the case of *Rhone v Stephens* (1994). The plaintiffs sued the defendant for the cost of repair to their leaking roof. Their cottage adjoined the defendant's home of which it had once been part. When the cottage was sold in 1960, the vendor (the owner of the adjoining house) covenanted for himself and his successors in title to 'maintain in good condition that part of the roof of the house which was above the cottage'. The plaintiffs acquired the cottage in 1981. When the roof subsequently leaked, the defendant tried to stop the leaks but failed. The defendant refused to allow the plaintiffs access to do the repairs themselves.

It was held that the covenant was a positive one and, therefore, not enforceable against a successor in title. It was affirmed that a positive covenant was not enforceable in equity against successors-in-title, nor was *Austerberry* (see below) overruled.

Lord Templeman said it had been accepted that equity would allow enforcement of negative covenants against freehold land, but there was no power to enforce positive ones against successors-in-title. He acknowledged the severe criticism of this position and that the Law Commission in 1965 had recommended the law be changed to allow positive covenants to run with the land, but if this were done and *Austerberry* overruled, it would 'create a number of difficulties, anomalies and uncertainties'.

Note

Under the Right of Access to Neighbouring Land Act 1992, the plaintiffs would probably have been granted access to repair.

The enforcement of the burden of a freehold covenant when the covenantee has transferred his land to another

This must be considered at common law and in equity.

The position at common law

The burden will not run (*Austerberry v Oldham Corporation* (1885)). This means that the covenantee cannot sue the successors-in-title of the covenantor. He can only sue the original party to the covenant, ie the original covenantor, and then only for damages because the original covenantor no longer owns the land so there cannot be specific performance. This means that if the original parties made an agreement whereby the covenantor agreed to restrict any building on his land to a bungalow and his successor-in-title built a multi-storey block of flats on it, the original covenantee could not get the flats removed and would only get damages for the breach of covenant (which may not be what he wants, eg if the flats mean he has lost his view).

The covenantor can protect himself against being sued for damages by one of the following:

- *Taking an indemnity covenant* from his successor-in-title at the time of the conveyance. This will enable him to sue his successor. Every time the burdened land is conveyed this can be done so that there is a chain of indemnity covenants. Unfortunately, this will be of no use if one successor-in-title in the chain goes missing.
- *By using the statutory device of the conveyance of a long lease,* ie by making a conveyance of a fee simple absolute for a term of years instead of a fee simple absolute in possession under s 153 of the Law of Property Act (LPA) 1925. The covenant then ceases to be a freehold covenant and becomes a leasehold one and the burdens of leasehold covenants run with the land under privity of estate (see Chapter 6, and the effect of LT(C)A 1995). There appear to be no cases where this has been used and it would appear to be a theoretical possibility only.
- *By using the rule in Halsall v Brizell or the doctrine of mutual benefit and burden* which means that where the covenantor receives a benefit he cannot refuse to take the burden as well. In *Halsall*, the benefit was the provision of roads, sewers, protection from flooding by the sea, etc. The burden was a contribution towards the cost of maintaining such services.

This rule enables even a positive covenant to be enforced and is an exception to the rule that positive covenants will never run with the land.

Of course, if a successor-in-title to the original covenantor does not take the benefit under the rule in *Halsall v Brizell*, he cannot be forced to take the burden, eg to contribute to payment for the maintenance of a private road which he never uses, because he walks across the fields to his house and has no car.

It may also be possible to use:

- *An analogy with Crow v Wood* (1971) where a boundary wall or fence is involved. In that case, a right in the nature of an easement involving the repair of a boundary fence or wall was upheld even though it meant expenditure.

- *Section 79 of the LPA 1925* on the basis that s 78 of the LPA 1925 was held in *Federated Homes v Mill Lodge Properties Ltd* (1981) to pass the benefit of a covenant unless there is a contrary expression in the deed. Some have held that this means s 79 should serve to pass the burden. It must be remembered, however, that *Federated Homes* has not yet been tested in the House of Lords and Lord Upjohn in *Topham Ltd v Earl of Sefton* (1966) stated that s 79 does not mean burdens run with the land (although this case was before *Federated Homes*).

  If, of course, s 79 does serve to pass the burdens of covenant then *Austerberry v Oldham Corporation* would not affect covenants made after 1925.

The position in equity

Under the rule in *Tulk v Moxhay* (1848) the burdens of covenants will run in equity if the following conditions are met:

- The covenant is negative in substance (*Haywood v Brunswick Benefit Building Society* (1881)).
- The covenant 'touches and concerns' the land. The test is the same as for *Swift Investments v Combined English Stores* (see Chapter 6 on Leasehold Covenants). It must not be personal in nature.
- The covenant must accommodate the dominant tenement, ie confer a benefit on land retained by the covenantee. At the date the covenant was made, the covenantee must have owned the dominant (ie benefited) land. In *London County Council v Allen* (1914), a covenant not to build on burdened land was held not to be enforceable because, at the time the covenant was made, the person who took the covenant (ie the covenantee) did not own the land to be benefited.
- The covenant must have been intended to run with the land. If s 79 of the LPA 1925 is interpreted to mean this is implied into all post-1925 covenants, then the covenant will run unless there is a specific term to the contrary.

Note

There are two exceptions to the rule in *Tulk v Moxhay* that the covenantee must retain land benefited by the covenant if the burden is to run:

- statutory exceptions where for reasons of public policy statute decrees the burden shall run, eg where the property concerned is National Trust property;
- where the covenants were made in conjunction with a building scheme (see Benefits below).

A recent case illustrating the position with regard to *positive* covenants was *Rhone v Stephens* (1994) above.

The enforceability of the benefit of freehold covenants

Again the position must be considered in several situations:

- where there are original parties;
- where statute is involved;
- at common law;
- in equity.

By the original parties

The original covenantee can always enforce the covenant for his benefited land against the original covenantor since there is privity of contract between them.

By statute

Section 56 of the LPA 1925 enables persons not actually named in the deed to enforce the benefit of a covenant against the original covenantor. This section states 'a person may ... take the benefit of any ... covenant or agreement over or respecting land ... although he may not be named as a party to the conveyance or other instrument'.

Such other persons, who are not party to the covenant deed, must be clearly identifiable and in existence (ie living) at the time the deed was made providing the benefit was intended to pass to them. This means that a covenant expressed to benefit 'the purchasers of Quiet Acre and the owners for the time being of Peace Haven Farm, their heirs and assigns' will benefit:

- the purchasers of Quiet Acre;
- the owners of Peace Haven Farm at present living.

However, it will not pass to benefit the heirs and assigns of Peace Haven Farm because they are neither identifiable (more may be born) nor yet in existence.

Amsprop Trading Ltd v Harris Distribution (1996) confirms that the persons within s 56 must be those with whom it was intended the covenant should be made.

At common law when the original covenantee has conveyed his land to a successor-in-title

The benefit of the covenant will run with the land so that the benefit passes to a successor-in-title if the following conditions are satisfied:

- The covenant touches and concerns the land.
- At the time the covenant was made, the covenantee must have held a legal estate in the land to be benefited.
- The covenant must have been intended to run with the land. Since *Smith and Snipes Hall Farm Ltd v R Douglas Catchment Board* (1949), s 78 of the LPA 1925 is deemed to satisfy this condition unless a contrary intention is expressed in the deed. This is because of the words 'that a covenant relating to any of the land of the covenantee shall be deemed to be made with the covenantee and his successors-in-title and the persons deriving title under him or them and shall have the same effect as if such successors and other persons were expressed'.
- The successor-in-title must hold the same legal estate as the original covenantee. *Smith and Snipes Hall Farm* has again modified this requirement. It is no longer necessary for the covenant to have been made between freeholders. The successor-in-title to the original covenantee may be a leaseholder. Section 78 of the LPA 1925 was held to have this effect.

The enforceability of the benefit of a freehold covenant in equity

When the four conditions governing the running of the benefit of a freehold covenant with the land at common law are not met, equity may enable it to run, eg where a successor-in-title to the original covenantee does not have a legal estate in the land but only an equitable one. Then, providing the covenant touches and concerns the land, the covenant may run in equity by one of the following methods:

- annexation;
- assignment;
- under a building scheme.

Annexation

Annexation is an attachment of the benefit to the dominant land. This may be by express, implied or statutory annexation.

Express annexation

Express annexation occurs when words in the deed expressly state that the benefit of the covenant shall run with the land and clearly identify the land to be so benefited.

In *Renals v Cowlishaw* (1878), the words, 'heirs, executors, administrators and assigns' were held to be insufficient to annex the benefit. There was no clear identification of the land to be benefited, 'assigns' did not identify the land; it could apply to the assignment of the benefit of the covenant rather than to the land itself.

In *Rogers v Hosegood* (1900), the words 'with the intent that the covenant might ... bind the premises thereby conveyed ... and might enure to the benefit of the vendors ... their heirs and assigns and others claiming under them' was held to be express annexation on the ground that not to allow this was to negate common sense; such intention was clear.

Note

Even if there are express words and the land is clearly identifiable, the courts have not always held there has been express annexation. In *Re Ballard's Conveyance* (1937), the express words were held to annex the benefit to only part of the dominant land.

It was held that this part could not be severed and since the express annexation was not applicable to all the land, the benefit could not run with the land.

Implied annexation

When circumstances make it clear there was an intention to annex the benefit of the covenant to the dominant land, such annexation will be implied.

In *Newton Abbot Cooperative Society v Williamson and Treadgold* (1952), the actual land to be benefited was not stated in the deed but it was clear that, since the covenant involved two shops opposite one another, one of which was an ironmongers called 'The Devonia', the Devonia was the property to be benefited. In the deed it was merely stated that the vendor lived at the Devonia.

In *Marten v Flight Refuelling Ltd* (1962), it was held that it would be contrary to common sense to rule against annexation and that annexation was implied.

Annexation by statute

The effect of the interpretation of s 78 of the LPA 1925 in *Federated Homes Ltd v Mill Lodge Properties* is to annex the benefit of a covenant, which touches and concerns the land, so that it runs with the land.

This interpretation has been heavily criticised and has not yet been tested in the House of Lords. (*Always* indicate this when referring to it in any question.)

This interpretation has not always been followed. *Roake v Chadka* (1984) concerned land sold by developers with a restrictive covenant that there should be no more than one house per plot.

In this case, there was a further clause that the benefit of this restrictive covenant should not run unless the conveyance expressly stated it was to do so. It was argued that the interpretation of s 78 of the LPA 1925 in *Federated Homes* meant that the benefit of the covenant ran with the land so that the owner of a plot who wanted to build a second house on it could not do so. It was held that he could. Section 78 could be interpreted to annexe the benefit of a covenant when the conveyance categorically stated that it would not run unless the conveyance expressly stated it was to do so. The agreement must be construed as a whole and the words 'unless the benefit of this covenant shall be expressly assigned' could not be discounted. There had been no annexation.

Federated Homes was also distinguished in *Sainsbury v Enfield BC* (1989). This concerned a restrictive covenant made in 1894. Sainsbury's wanted a declaration that it was no longer enforceable. It was held that this was the case; the covenant was not enforceable.

The 1894 conveyance had not annexed the benefit and s 78 of the LPA 1925 did not apply. For covenants made before 1925 there must be words which result in express or implied annexation.

Assignment

Where the benefit of a covenant has not been annexed to the land, it may run through express assignment, providing the following conditions are met:

- the covenant must have been taken for the benefit of the land of the covenantee;
- the land to be benefited must be clearly identifiable (considered in *Newton Abbot Cooperative Society* (above));
- the covenant must be assigned at the same time the conveyance is made. A covenant made after the conveyance will not serve to pass the benefit (*Re Union of London and Smith's Bank Ltd Conveyance* (1993));
- there must be an unbroken chain of such assignments so that the benefit of the covenant is passed to the new owner of the land. An assignment, unlike annexation, attaches the benefit to the person, not to the land (*Re Pinewood Estate, Farnborough* (1958)).

Building scheme

When a developer has a building scheme or development plan and sells off plots to individuals, he may take covenants from these plot buyers, giving a benefit to the land he is developing. Under such a scheme or plan, the benefit of these covenants is then transferred to all other plot purchasers and their successors in title. This means that all the owners of the houses which are built may enforce the covenants and maintain the estate as the developer envisaged, eg if X buys a house with a covenant not to fence off his front garden, all the owners of houses within the development, and their successors-in-title, may sue him for breach of covenant if he does.

The requirements for such a scheme were laid down in *Elliston v Reacher* (1908):

- there must be a development plan in existence before any plot is sold and this plan must show the layout of the plots and show the total area involved;
- the developer must be the common vendor for all the plots so that all those buying a plot derive title from this common vendor;
- every plot must be subject to the same restrictions at the time the plot is sold, and it must be clear that these restrictions were intended to benefit the whole scheme, ie all the plots were to be subject to the restriction not only for the immediate purchasers but also for their successors-in-title;
- every purchaser must have bought his plot knowing that the covenants were intended to benefit all the plots in the scheme, in other words, to be mutually binding.

These conditions have now been modified, as the following cases illustrate.

In *Baxter v Four Oaks Properties Ltd* (1965), the original scheme allowed houses to be of different sizes and prices but all were subject to a covenant restricting each to being a private dwelling.

Despite the different sizes and the lack of any evidence that the estate was laid out in a plan before any plot was sold, it was held that it constituted a building scheme and that there was an intention there should be mutually enforceable covenants.

In *Re Dolphin's Conveyance* (1970), there was no common vendor, nor a pre-existing plan, before the plots were sold. It was held that there was a common intention when the covenants were taken so that the identical covenants taken by each plot owner were enforceable under a building scheme.

In *Brunner v Greenslade* (1971), a purchaser of only *part* of a plot was held to be able to enforce a covenant against all other plot-holders in the building scheme.

Note

In *Emile Elias v Pine Groves* (1993) a part of an estate was divided into five plots. These were sold to four purchasers. On a plan, plot 5 was annexed to the conveyance of plots 4 and 5 but the general plan did not show plot 5 annexed to the other plots. Each purchaser covenanted with the vendor and his assigns that they would not build anything but one dwelling house on each plot. The covenants taken by the purchasers of plots 2 and 3 were not quite the same as those taken by the other purchasers. The division into plots took place in 1938 but in 1948 the developers executed a deed with the four owners of the five plots whereby the owner of plots 4 and 5 was released from the covenant not to build more than one house on plots 4 and 5 (which were combined). There was no other release in the deed.

Later plot 3 was purchased by the plaintiff and plot 1 by the defendant. The defendant then began to erect houses on the land and the plaintiff sought to enforce the covenant to restrict him to one house. It was held that he could not. There had been no building scheme in 1938 no chain of assignments, and no express annexation to pass the benefit of the restrictive covenant. There was never a defined plan to ensure that all the original purchasers knew there was a scheme and the area it covered. Plot 5 had never been shown annexed to the conveyances of plots 1, 2 and 3. Neither were the covenants all the same.

This means for a building scheme, there must be an identifiable scheme and a common intention that the covenants should be enforceable by all the purchasers.

The modification and discharge of restrictive covenants

Restrictive covenants endure indefinitely, unless they have been discharged, but once terminated they cannot be enforced by anyone; neither by the original covenantee nor his successor-in-title.

Covenants may be released by either:
- release; or
- merger; or
- the Lands Tribunal.

Discharge by release

The only person who can release a covenant is the person entitled to the benefit, ie the covenantee and he may do so by express release or conduct.

Discharge by express release

This is discharge by deed or by acquiescence, expressly ignoring the breach.

In *Shaw v Applegate* (1977), a property was converted for use as an amusement arcade in contravention of a restrictive covenant. The covenantee had acquiesced to it. The court refused to grant an injunction to enforce the covenant but did award damages against the original covenantor.

Discharge by conduct

This is where the covenant is impliedly released because it would be inequitable, in view of the circumstances, to enforce it.

In *Chatsworth Estates v Fewell* (1931), the estate owners took covenants from all the purchasers of their sea-front properties in Eastbourne that the properties should not be used other than as 'private dwelling houses'. Over the years, several houses had become schools, flats and boarding houses. The defendant wished to use his house as a boarding house.

It was held that the estate had taken no action against these other breaches of covenant so it would be inequitable to allow this to be enforced.

Discharge by merger

When the two properties, that carrying the burden and that enjoying the benefit, come under a single owner, the covenants are extinguished (*Texaco Antilles Ltd v Kernochan* (1973)). The position is the same as in easement.

Discharge by application to the Lands Tribunal

Section 84(1) of the LPA 1925 gives the Lands Tribunal a discretionary power to modify or discharge restrictive covenants, with or without compensation, under one of the following conditions:

* 'change in the character of the property or neighbourhood or any other circumstances which make it obsolete'; or

- that 'reasonable use of land for public or private purposes' would be impeded; or
- that the persons entitled to the benefit of the covenant have agreed to its discharge or modification impliedly or expressly; or
- the person entitled to the benefit of the covenant will 'not be injured' if it is modified or discharged.

A person wishing to have the covenant discharged must apply to the tribunal but will, in all cases, have to prove that one of the above conditions exists and that the person entitled to the benefit will be adequately compensated by money.

Discharge is not easily obtained even when planning permission has been granted, eg *Re Martin's Application* (1989) where it was stated that a planning decision is not a basis for extinguishing a covenant.

In *Re Beech's Application* (1990), a former council house which had been sold to existing tenants was subject to a covenant that it should not be used other than as a dwelling house. Planning permission was later given for its use as an office and application made to the Land Tribunal under s 84(1) for discharge of the covenant. It was refused and the refusal was upheld by the Court of Appeal. The ground for refusal was the fear that it would lead to other applications and thus the residential nature of the area would be destroyed.

Cf the most recent case: *Re Lloyds and Lloyds Application* (1993). The subject was a restrictive covenant that no trade or business should be carried on and no intoxicating liquors allowed on the property (a house). The owners had obtained planning permission to turn it into a community home for psychiatric patients and contended that the character of the neighbourhood had changed sufficiently to allow this. The house next door had become a building business property and there was a home for the aged nearby. This meant that there would be no effect of devaluing neighbouring properties.

It was held that the change in the neighbourhood was insufficient to deem the covenant obsolete. On the other hand, it was government policy to provide homes for old people and there was a desperate need for such homes in the community. The covenant was contrary to this policy and this need. The owners had been deemed suitable to run such a home and there was no evidence that the use would be any more objectionable than that of the schools or the boarding house already in the area. The court allowed modification of the covenant.

However, in *Re Wallace and Co's Application* (1993), planning permission had been given for the erection of eight garages on land subject to a restrictive covenant not to allow any building on the land. It was held that the covenant could not be modified or discharged. It was not obsolete as far as the interests of neighbours were concerned. The loss of an open space could not be compensated for in money.

In *Re the Gate House and Stable Block, Kingswood Cottage Stables* (1996), there was an application for the modification of a restrictive covenant under s 84 of the LPA 1925. Owners of Kingswood Lodge, adjoining freehold land called Kingswood Cottage, objected to the conversion of part of the cottage stables into a one-bedroomed building. The two properties had been in one ownership until 1985 and when the cottage was sold it was with a restrictive covenant that no trade or business should be carried on there, nor any building be used other than as a private dwelling or stable for horses.

It was held that though there would be no loss of privacy to the lodge and there would only be a marginal affect in terms of noise and activity and little change in the character of the neighbourhood, the covenant was a valuable benefit to the objectors so the requirements of s 84 were not satisfied. This was not a case where public interest overrode private objections. There would be no modification allowed.

In two recent cases, the Lands Tribunal has allowed modification. In *Re Land Adjoining Merton Road, Slough* (1996), there was a restrictive covenant preventing the erection of a block of flats. A house which had become somewhat derelict was subject to this restriction. It formed part of an earlier development scheme which contained one plot on which the covenant had been different in that it allowed the erection of two semi-detached houses or two self-contained flats. The tribunal allowed modification to allow four one-bedroomed flats and four two-bedroomed flats to replace the house provided they were within a two-storeyed building of similar size. There had been no objections to the application.

In *Re 8, Acacia Road, Hordle* (1996), the Tribunal allowed a modification of a restrictive covenant restricting building to one house per plot to allow an additional house.

Note

In *Brown v Heathland Mental NHS Trust* (1996), an estate was subject to a covenant that no premises on it should be used other than as a private dwelling house. Residents therefore applied for an injunction to prevent a property on the estate, which the trust had bought, from being used to house five mental patients.

It was held that the trust was a body set up by Parliament under the NHS and Community Care Act 1990 and that it had acquired the property to carry out its statutory functions. The benefit of a restrictive covenant could not stand in the way as established in *Re Elms Avenue*

(1948). The fact that the property had been acquired by voluntary agreement rather than compulsion did not affect the position. The land is not freed from the restrictive covenant but the restriction cannot be enforced by an action against a statutory body which has acquired the land. Those deprived of the benefit may apply for compensation under s 10 of the Compulsory Purchase Act 1965.

The protection of restrictive covenants

Restrictive covenants may be registered whether they concern registered or unregistered land.

Registered land

The covenant must be registered as a minor interest against the owner of the burdened land by a notice or caution. This must be done before a purchaser buys this burdened land.

Note

Notice is only effective against the *purchaser* of the burdened land; if the land is *given* to someone, then the burden remains with the land regardless of whether or not the covenant is registered. Similarly, the burden remains if the land is acquired by adverse possession.

If the burdened land does not have the covenant registered as a minor interest, then the covenant is unenforceable against a purchaser of it.

Unregistered land

A restrictive covenant may be registered as a Class D(ii) land charge against the name of the original covenantor under the Land Charges Act (LCA) 1972. If it is so registered, then any purchaser of the land bearing the burden will be bound by it.

As in the case of registered land, registration only applies to purchasers. A gift of the land serves to transfer the burden of the covenant, whether or not it was registered as a land charge.

If the covenant is not so registered *before* the original covenantor sells the land, it will not be enforceable against any future purchaser even if the purchaser knew of the covenant before he purchased the land. This is the effect of s 3(6) of the LCA 1972 (see Chapter 2).

If the covenant was made before 1926, the doctrine of notice applies. It is not registrable.

Reform of the law on covenants

There have been several committees which have considered this, the most recent being the 1984 Committee.

The 1984 Law Commission on freehold covenants

The 1984 Law Commission on Freehold Covenants was set up to resolve the difficulties and differences in the running of the burdens of freehold covenants, particularly the fact that the burdens of positive covenants will not run either at common law or in equity, whereas the burdens of negative covenants will run in equity under *Tulk v Moxhay* (1848). In its Report No 127 published in 1985 it proposed:

- An entirely new interest in land to be called a 'land obligation' to be akin to an easement with a dominant land to be benefited and a servient land to be burdened.
- Such land obligations could be either positive or negative.
- Land obligations would be of two types:
  (a) A 'neighbour obligation'. These would comprise existing covenants whether positive or negative.
  (b) A 'development obligation' where owners of integrated property units shared common obligations and rights.
- The land obligations could be legal or equitable. A legal obligation would be made by deed either for a term of years absolute or for a fee simple absolute in possession. Equitable obligations would be made in writing but not require a deed. All land obligations would be registrable for unregistered land as a Class C land charge and for registered land registered against the titles of both the dominant and the servient land.
- The Law Commission further suggested that if the original covenantor transferred his land to a successor-in-title he should no longer be liable if there was a breach of the obligation. This means that an obligation would only be enforceable by the actual owner of the benefited land at the time of the breach, against the actual owner of the burdened land.

Question hints

- Make sure the original covenants were between freeholders (different rules apply to leasehold covenants).
- Identify the covenantor and the covenantee.
- Where there are several conveyances it may be helpful to draw a quick diagram, indicating changes as in the diagram below.

William owns both

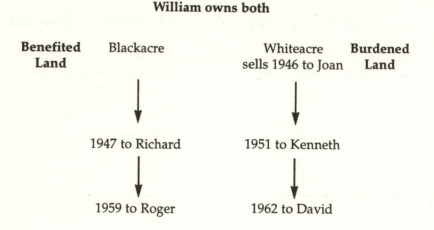

Benefited Land	Blackacre	Whiteacre sells 1946 to Joan	**Burdened Land**
	1947 to Richard	1951 to Kenneth	
	1959 to Roger	1962 to David	

Then add any date(s) of other dealings with the land, eg registration. Remember, if the covenant is not registered against the burdened land before it is sold, the covenant will be void as against a *purchaser*.

- Is the covenant positive (burden will not pass) or negative (burden passed in equity)? Remember *Crow v Wood* (1971) for fences or walls but also the latest case *Rhone v Stephens* (1994).
- Consider the benefits and burdens separately but remember ss 78 and 79 of the LPA 1925 do not apply to covenants made before 1926, so do not use *Federated Homes Ltd v Mill Lodge Properties Ltd* (1980) for these. Indicate, if you do refer to the interpretation of s 78 as able to pass the benefit, that the interpretation made in *Federated Homes* has not been tested in the House of Lords; and if you indicate s 79 may serve to pass the burden by analogy with the interpretation of s 78, that this is subject to debate and many would not accept it, eg Lord Upjohn.

- Is there a purchaser each time the land is conveyed? Or is it a gift or is there an adverse possessor? Has the covenant been protected?
- Does the person you are advising want a remedy? If so, what? Can he get specific performance?

9 Adverse possession

> **You should be familiar with the following areas:**
> - The Limitation Act 1980
> - meaning of adverse possession
> - time of accrual
> - position on expiry of limitation period

Squatting, as adverse possession is colloquially called, is an act of trespass. Trespass is a criminal act under the new Criminal Justice Bill so that the law on adverse possession may be affected.

The Limitation Act 1980

This governs the present position. Section 15 of the Limitation Act (LA) 1980 prevents a legal title holder from bringing an action to recover possession of his land more than 12 years after it was first adversely possessed, ie after 12 years the legal title holder becomes time-barred from taking any action.

There are, however, certain exceptions to this:

- For Crown Lands which have been adversely possessed the period is 30 years.

Note
Where the legal title holder is trying to repossess land adversely possessed by the Crown, the limitation period is the normal one of 12 years.

- Where the land involved is settled land, whether settled under a strict settlement or a trust for sale. In such cases there are two limitation periods:

(a) six years from the death of the last life tenant, ie after the date at which the remainderman comes into possession; or

(b) 12 years' adverse possession when there is a life tenant.

- Where the land is held under a lease, the freeholder may gain possession when the lease determines. If he does not, and the land remains adversely possessed, then the limitation period begins to accrue against the freeholder from the time the lease did determine.

Note
Determination may not be by reversion to the freeholder at end of lease term. A lease may be determined by surrender or, where a right of re-entry has been reserved, by breach of covenant.

Incapacity
This is where the true owner cannot exercise possession, for example, where he or she is a patient under Mental Health Act 1983. In this case, time accrues from six weeks after he or she ceases to be disabled or dies, but only if he or she was disabled at the time the adverse possession began. If he or she became disabled after the adverse possession started, then the usual 12 year period applies.

Acknowledgment of title holder
This prevents a claim for adverse possession. In *Edgington v Clark* (1967), a squatter occupied a bomb site in London for seven years. He then decided to try to buy it. Sale was refused. After a further 10 years, making a total of 17 years' occupation, he claimed adverse possession.

It was held that he could not claim adverse possession. When he offered to buy the land, he acknowledged the legal title holder's claim to it. His claim for adverse possession could only accrue from the time he made his offer to buy, so he had not satisfied the 12 years' limitation period, and the title owner was not time-barred from recovering his land.

Numerous squatters
Where there are numerous squatters succeeding one another without a break in between, the period of adverse possession accrues from the time the first of the squatters adversely possessed the land, provided that at no time during the 12 year period any of them attempted to acquire the land legally (*Mount Carmel Investments Ltd v Peter Thurlow Ltd* (1988)).

The time from which adverse possession begins to accrue

What is adverse possession is a matter of case law. In *Wallis's Cayton Bay Holiday Camp Ltd v Shell Mex & BP Ltd* (1975), it was held to occur when:

- the true owner 'had discontinued possession' or had been dispossessed; and
- the adverse possessor had taken the land adversely. This means something like ouster of the true owner had occurred.

In *Treloar v Nute* (1976), discontinuance by the paper owner, or his dispossession and 'ouster' of him, was again held to be required. In this instance, the owner of a partly derelict farm was held to be dispossessed when the defendant and his son used the land for grazing, improved it, and fenced it so that it was included within their boundaries. After 12 years they began to build upon it. It was held that these acts were sufficient to constitute adverse possession and it was clear their intention was to dispossess the true owner.

Intention of the true owner

On the other hand, in *Leigh v Jack* (1879), there was held to be no adverse possession because the true owner could not have been dispossessed. There was an intention the land should be a road.

The question of intention was also raised in *Wallis's Cayton Bay* where an intention on the part of the true owner to use the land claimed (by the adverse possessor) as a garage, was regarded as evidence that he had not abandoned the land nor discontinued possession.

Intention by the adverse possessor

Intention to both dispossess the true owner and to take possession must be evinced by the adverse possessor.

In *Powell v McFarlane* (1977), the adverse possessor had cut hay from the true owner's land. He had also grazed his animals on it and sold trees from it as Christmas trees. In addition, he had repaired the broken fences.

These acts were not held to be sufficient proof of his intention to possess the land and oust the true owner. *Animus possiendi* involves 'the intention ... to exclude the world at large' (Slade LJ).

Note

Long v Tower Hamlets LBC (1996): if a squatter has been given a lease, then he cannot claim adverse possession, providing the lease is granted by the owner of the land.

In *Mulcahy v Curramore Pty Ltd* (1974), the erection of a fence by an adverse possessor was held to be evidence of occupation by him and 'useful' as signifying his intention to exclude everyone else.

On the other hand, in *Fruin v Fruin* (1983), a fence was held not to be evidence of an intention to dispossess the true owner because its true purpose was to prevent a senile member of the family from straying.

Note

Cockburn LJ in *Sneddon v Smith* (1877) held enclosure to be the 'strongest possible evidence of adverse possession'.

Lord Hagan in *The Lord Advocate v Lord Lovat* (1888) held that the 'acts implying possession in one case may be totally inadequate in another'.

In *Hughes v Cork* (1994), enclosure was held to be the most cogent evidence of adverse possession and dispossession of the true owner.

The present situation

The whole subject was reviewed and clarified in *Buckinghamshire County Council v Moran* (1989).

Moran had taken adverse possession of a strip of land abutting his property and, regarding it as part of his garden, had planted it with daffodils and other bulbs. The title owners contended that they had never relinquished possession so Moran could not have acquired it by adverse possession. The court tried to bring certainty to the law by enumerating the conditions required for adverse possession, namely:

- an intention to possess the land must be evinced by the adverse possessor but this does not, of necessity, require an intention to acquire the legal title;
- the possession took place after the true owner had been dispossessed or had abandoned the land;
- there has been 12 years' adverse possession so that the paper owner is time barred from action under s 15 of the LA 1980.

In this case, Moran was deemed to have acquired adverse possession when he treated the strip as part of his garden and had shown an intention to dispossess the legal owner. Slade LJ said:

It is hard to see what more he could have done to acquire complete physical control of the plot ... he had plainly acquired factual possession.

The position when the limitation period has expired

This differs according to whether the land is registered or unregistered.

Unregistered land

Under s 17 of the LA 1980 the title of the paper owner is extinguished.

Note
If the land is leasehold, then the leaseholder's title is extinguished but not that of the freeholder. Time does not begin to run against the free-holder until the lease has determined, either by elapse of the lease term or by surrender of the lease or by re-entry for breach of covenant, where this is a term of the lease. This was established in *Fairweather v St Marylebone Property Co Ltd* (1963). This means that a leaseholder may regain possession and then make a new lease to the original leaseholder.

Registered land

Unlike the title of the paper title holder in unregistered land, the title of the paper title holder in registered land is not extinguished. In this situation, the paper title holder holds his title on trust for the adverse possessor (s 75 of the LA 1980). He cannot remove the squatter who has acquired, by his adverse possession, an overriding interest under s 70(1)(f) of the Land Registration Act (LRA) 1925 as 'a right acquired or in the course of being acquired' under the LA 1980.

What the adverse possessor should do

Having established that the legal title owner is time-barred under s 15 of the LA 1980 from bringing an action for repossession, the adverse possessor should seek to register the interest he has now acquired in the land.

If the land is unregistered

The squatter should apply to the Land Registry for registration as proprietor of the adversely possessed land. He will be registered as proprietor of a possessory title, ie a title of the lowest grade, but if he has been registered as such for 12 years and is in possession of the land, or if the Registrar is satisfied his claim is valid, the Registrar may upgrade it. Where the land is leasehold, registration will be limited to the period of the lease.

If the land is registered

The squatter should apply for rectification of the register under s 82(1) of the LRA 1925. Rectification gives effect to the overriding interest the adverse possessor has acquired under s 70(1)(f) of the LRA 1925 (*Chowood v Lyall* (1930)). The squatter will then become the registered proprietor; and the paper title holder may not be indemnified when this takes place, because it is deemed he has suffered no loss. This is because the squatter's overriding interest was in existence before the rectification took place (*Re Chowood's Registered Land* (1993)). Until rectification the paper title owner holds his title on trust for the squatter.

If the land is leasehold, rectification means the lessee's title is no longer appropriate he no longer appears on the register of proprietors because the lease in practical terms becomes vested in the adverse possessor. This means that the lessee of the paper title can no longer determine his lease by surrender, so the freeholder cannot regain possession as he can in the case of unregistered land (*Spectrum Investment v Holmes* (1981)). Only the squatter can surrender the lease. This raises the problem of whether the original lessee is bound by a lease he no longer holds.

Note

The adverse possessor is not a purchaser so that any third party rights will be protected even if they are not registered. This is because they are only void if not registered against a *purchaser* for valuable consideration (*Re Nisbet and Potts Contract* (1906)). This is why an unregistered covenant can be enforced against a squatter.

The adverse possessor must not acknowledge the paper owner's legal title even after the 12 year period has elapsed

It has always been held that any recognition of the legal title holder to the property by the adverse possessor before 12 years has elapsed has meant that the 12 year period must begin to accrue again.

Colchester Borough Council v Smith (1992) seems to have extended this to include recognition *after* the 12 years. A written acknowledgment of such title during negotiations over a dispute was ruled to mean the adverse possessor had not satisfied the requirements of s 15 of the LA 1980.

10 Mortgages

You should be familiar with the following areas:

- legal mortgages
- equitable mortgages
- redemption of mortgages
- rights of the mortgagor
- rights of the mortgagee
- mortgages and the Consumer Credit Act 1974
- priority of mortgages

Definition

A mortgage is 'A transaction under which land or chattels are given as security, for the payment of a debt or discharge of some obligation' (*Santley v Wilde* (1899) *per* Lindley MR).

The person who lends the money is the mortgagee. The person who borrows the money is the mortgagor. A mortgage gives the mortgagee an interest in the property but, in fact, most of what are called mortgages are really charges on property which give the mortgagee certain rights over it but no proprietary rights in it.

Mortgages may be legal or equitable.

Legal mortgages

There are two types: of the fee simple, and of a term of years absolute.

Legal mortgage of the fee simple
Legal mortgages of the fee simple (ie of freehold land) are covered by two sub-divisions of s 85 of the Law of Property Act (LPA) 1925:

- A demise for a term of years absolute subject to provision for cessor on redemption. Before 1926 this involved the transfer of the estate with provision for re-transfer back to the mortgagor if the mortgage was repaid on the date agreed. This is no longer the case.

  Section 85(2) ensures there can no longer be a transfer of the fee simple; any purported transfer is made into a lease for 3,000 years beginning when the mortgage is taken out.

  Should there be a second mortgage taken out on the same property, it must be one day longer than the term of the first mortgage.

  Example

  X owns Blackacre in fee simple. He mortgages it to Y for 50 years. He needs more cash 10 years later so he mortgages it to Z.

  The mortgage term for this second mortgage to Z must be at least 40 years and one day. This is so that Y, the first mortgagee, can get his money back first.

- A charge by deed expressed to be by way of legal mortgage comes within s 87 of the LPA 1925. Here, no length of term of the mortgage is specified; there is only a charge with provision for repayment. This is the usual building society mortgage arrangement but there is usually a clause which does indicate the length of the mortgage term. Section 87(1) makes it clear that where there is such a charge, the mortgagee is in the same position as regards protection, powers and remedies as if there were a mortgage term of 3,000 years.

Legal mortgages for a term of years absolute

With legal mortgages for a term of years absolute, ie for leasehold land; there again two sub-divisions.

- By a legal mortgage under a sub-lease for a term of years absolute. The sub-lease term must be less than the unexpired term of the mortgagor's lease. Section 86(2) requires this to be at least 10 days less and again there must be provision for cessor on redemption.

  Should a second mortgage be taken out, this must be at least one day longer than that of the first mortgage term.

  Example

  John has a lease for 99 years. He mortgages it to B. John's lease has an unexpired term of 60 years so he mortgages it to B for a term of 60 years less 10 days, ie for 59 years, 355 days, with the proviso that the lease will revert to him on repayment of the loan. John is still in financial difficulties, so he raises a second mortgage on this same land by granting Gerald a sub-lease for a term which is at least one day longer than that of B's term, ie for 59 years, 356 days.

- By a charge by deed expressed to be by way of legal mortgage. This means by the same method as for the legal mortgage of a fee simple absolute. Raising a mortgage by a charge by deed is preferred by most building societies and banks because it makes it easier for the mortgagor to understand, and both freehold and leasehold properties can be dealt with together.

Equitable mortgages

There are four methods of creation.

A contract to create a legal mortgage

This becomes an equitable mortgage because of the maxim 'Equity regards as done that which ought to be done'.

It must be in writing if it is made after 25 September 1989 to comply with s 2 of the Law of Property (Miscellaneous Provisions) Act (LP(MP)A) 1989 amending s 40 of the LPA 1925 (or be 'manifested and proved' in writing if made before that date, and supported by part performance) and the mortgage money must have been paid to the mortgagor.

A mortgage by deposit of title deeds

This is an informal mortgage where the title deeds are intended as security for the loan. A written memorandum is not necessary though desirable. However, since s 2 of the LP(MP)A 1989, it seems that this method can no longer be used, though there is some confusion about the position.

But

In *United Bank of Kuwait v Sahib* (1994), the mere deposit of title deeds was ineffective to create an equitable mortgage in the absence of a written contract which satisfies s 2 of the LP(MP)A 1989.

An equitable charge

This is rare. It arises where an owner charges his land by means of an agreement in writing, stating that it is intended to be for repayment of a loan.

An equitable mortgage of an equitable interest

An equitable interest cannot be the subject of a legal mortgage. The mortgage must be in writing but there is no requirement of a deed.

A tenant for life can make an equitable mortgage of his equitable interest; so can a beneficiary under a trust for sale.

Redemption of a mortgage

The right to redeem a mortgage may be at common law, or in equity.

The right to redeem at common law

This is a matter of contract so the mortgagor has the right to redeem on the date stated in the contract and on that date only, neither before nor after. In the past, if the mortgage was not redeemed on that due date, the mortgagee took the land and the mortgagor could still be sued for the repayment of the debt.

The right to redeem in equity

Equity intervenes to mitigate the undesirable effects of common law and gives the mortgagor a right to redeem on reasonable terms, even if the date for redemption fixed by the contract has passed or not yet arrived. For this reason, the legal date of redemption is usually fixed at six months after the date on which the mortgage was created, even though neither mortgagor nor mortgagee expect redemption at that date. This method is used so that the mortgagee will have the usual remedies available to him should the mortgagor break the terms of the mortgage deed.

The rights of the mortgagor

The borrower's (mortgagor's) rights in total, form the equity of redemption, ie a total bundle of rights which give him an interest in the land as distinct from an interest in its redemption. Such equitable interest arises as soon as the mortgage is created.

Note
Do not confuse the equity of redemption, ie the total bundle of rights with the equitable right to redeem, which is the equitable right associated only with the date of redemption.

The *equity of redemption* includes:
- the equitable right to redeem;
- the right to be free of any unconscionable or oppressive terms;
- the right to be free of any collateral agreements favouring the mortgage;
- the right to be free of undue influence.

The right to redeem

'Once a mortgage, always a mortgage', it can never be anything else, so there must be a right to redeem. Anything which makes redemption illusory will be declared void, so there must be:

- no clogs or letters preventing redemption;
- no postponement of the date of redemption.

The right to redeem must be free of any clogs or fetters
The following cases illustrate this.

In *Samuel v Jarrah Timber and Woodpaving Corpn Ltd* (1904), P agreed to lend money to the Timber Company on the security of company stock providing he was given an option to purchase most of the stock, at a given price, within 12 months. There was a clause in the agreement that the advance was to become due and payable with interest at 30 days notice on either side. Before the 12 months had elapsed, the mortgagors gave notice of their wish to repay the loan. P then sought to exercise his option. It was held that the option was void, it prevented the mortgagor's right to redeem.

In the case of *Reeve v Lisle* (1902), there were two agreements, a mortgage deed and a separate agreement giving the mortgagee an option to purchase the property. The agreements had been made 10 days apart, the option agreement being the later one. The court held that both agreements were valid.

The difference in the two cases lies in the fact that in *Samuel* the agreements were made together so that the option could be construed as unconscionable; the mortgagor could have felt bound to accept the option in order to obtain the mortgage – this was not so in *Reeve* where the option was agreed 10 days after the mortgage agreement. There was no clog on the equity of redemption.

No postponement of the date of redemption
Any attempt to postpone redemption will be regarded as inequitable and clauses to this effect declared void if they make redemption illusory.

Knightsbridge Estates Trust Ltd v Bryne (1940) concerned a mortgage term of 40 years with a clause that one default in respect of mortgage instalments would mean the principal sum and interest would become immediately payable. The mortgagor then found he could get a cheaper mortgage elsewhere and sought to redeem claiming it was a fetter on his right to redeem.

The court decided that he could not. There was no clog on the equity of redemption, the terms were not inequitable.

Fairclough v Swan Brewery Co Ltd (1912) concerned a mortgage on a property with a 20 year lease. There was 17½ years of the lease left to run. There was a clause which would not allow the mortgagor to redeem until six weeks before the lease was due to expire.

This mortgage was meant to be irredeemable for all practical purposes. He would have got back only six weeks of his lease, this would be of no advantage to him.

The right to be free of oppressive or unconscionable terms

Note

Oppressive or unconscionable does not mean unreasonable but morally reprehensible. Usually such terms are concerned with interest rates. A high interest rate is not necessarily oppressive. It depends on the circumstances; consider the following cases.

In *Cityland and Property (Holdings) Ltd v Dabrah* (1968), D was a tenant who took out a loan in order to buy the freehold of his house. He faced the possibility of eviction when his lease expired if he did not buy. He borrowed the money from his landlord, but the landlord imposed a 'premium' instead of an interest rate. This meant that he would pay a high price for the purchase and when this was calculated as an interest rate it turned out to be around 12%.

The agreement was held to be unconscionable since 7% would have been a fair interest rate; it was clear the parties were not equal in bargaining power.

In *Multiservice Bookbinding Ltd v Marden* (1979), mortgage terms were agreed in terms of the Swiss Franc. The pound declined in value against the Swiss Franc so that the mortgagor was paying back far more than be bargained for.

It was held there were no oppressive or unconscionable terms and index-linked agreements were valid. (See also *Woodstead Finance Ltd v Petrou* (1986) and *A Ketley Ltd v Scott* (1981) on p 141.)

The right to be free of disadvantageous collateral agreements

This means that there must be no other advantages the mortgagee makes for himself when he gives a mortgage. These advantages are often contained in agreements restraining the mortgagor from freely trading with whom he pleases. The court's attitude to such agreements was very strict in the old cases, particularly if the restraint clause is not restricted to the length of the mortgage term.

In *Biggs v Hoddinott* (1898), a mortgage contained a clause that during the five year mortgage, D would purchase beer only from P, and that the mortgage could not be redeemed for five years nor would the mortgagees end it for five years. The five year term was held to be reasonable.

Compare *Noakes and Co Ltd v Rice* (1902), which concerned the mortgage of a lease of a public house, with a clause that the mortgagor would purchase beer only from the mortgagee's brewery for the whole term of the lease, not just for the term of the mortgage. D wanted to redeem the mortgage and become a free house.

It was held that the clause was a clog or fetter on the equity of redemption. The maximum 'once a mortgage always a mortgage' applied.

In *Bradley v Carritt* (1866) a shareholder mortgaged his shares in a tea company. The agreement involved him in doing his best to ensure that the mortgagee would always be the tea company's broker. If the tea company did not use him as such, the mortgagor would pay the mortgagee all the commission he would have had if the tea company had used him.

The clause was said to be a fetter on the equity of redemption. D could redeem the mortgage and become a free house.

The position has been modified since these cases to take into account the principles of bargains made for commercial purposes, which, if not unconscionable, should stand.

In *Krelginger v New Patagonia Meat and Cold Storage Co Ltd* (1914), a meat company mortgaged its property to a wool broker with an agreement that, for five years, the meat company would offer its sheep skins to the mortgagees who would purchase them if they wished to do so at market price. Two years later the meat company wished to redeem its mortgage, and with it, the commitment to offer sheep skins to the mortgagees.

The court held that the five year term for the option was valid and the agreement was reasonable because it was limited to a short time and the skins were to be purchased at best market price. The mortgagor could not redeem the mortgage; the mortgage and option were separate agreements. There was no clog or fetter on the equity of redemption.

Note

Agreements which are in restraint of trade will not be upheld if they are unreasonable.

In *Esso Petroleum Co Ltd v Harper's Garage (Southport) Ltd* (1968), Esso made agreements with two garages owned by D to sell only Esso lines. One agreement was for four and a half years; the agreement with the second garage was for 21 years and this was a collateral agreement to a mortgage of 21 years. The agreement with the second garage was to run with the mortgage term.

The term of five years was held to be reasonable; the term of 21 years with the second garage was unreasonable and therefore void. The fact that there was a mortgage did not mean the restraint of trade principle could not be invoked.

Alec Lobb Garages (Ltd) v Total Oil GB Ltd (1985) referred to *Esso Petroleum* and reaffirmed that where there was a clause requiring a trader to take supplies solely from one company, the crucial factor is the length of time the agreement is to last; five years is reasonable.

The right to be free of undue influence

There has been a claw-back from *Lloyd's Bank Ltd v Bundy* (1975) when Lord Denning suggested that a mere inequality in bargaining powers of mortgagee and mortgagor was sufficient to raise the possibility of undue influence. In *National Westminster bank plc v Morgan* (1985) two conditions were deemed necessary:

- that the mortgagor could show he had been victimised or the mortgagee had gained an unfair advantage; and
- the circumstances of the relationship were so inequitable that they could only have arisen because of undue influence.

It was clear that the mere existence of a relationship such as that of husband and wife, or bank and customer could not lead to a presumption there would be undue influence.

In *Kings North Trust Ltd v Bell* (1986), W had signed the mortgage deed for a mortgage on the matrimonial home in which she had a beneficial interest, her husband being the legal title owner. Her husband had lied to her stating it was a non-risk, short-term loan only.

The court held that the trust company had left it to the husband to explain to his wife and to obtain her signature so that he became the company's agent. This meant they were bound by his misrepresentation and, therefore, Mrs Bell's right took priority over those of the company.

It was made clear in *CIBC Mortgages plc v Pitt* (1993) by the House of Lords that:

- If a mortgagee had actual or constructive notice of undue influence being exerted, or if the person exerting such influence was an agent of the mortgagee, then the mortgagee himself would be regarded as exerting undue influence.
- Where a person signs a mortgage as security for their spouse or cohabitee as in *Barclays Bank v O'Brien* (1992), a mortgagee will be deemed to have had constructive notice of undue influence, because there is always a risk of it in such cases, even if it is not actually present; but when a person signs as a joint mortgagor (as in *CIBC Mortgages v Pitt*) for a mortgage to them as co-owners of the property, there will be deemed to be no constructive notice of such influence.
- Where the mortgagee has notice of undue influence, he must be able to show what steps he took to ensure the claimant was given independent advice.

Note
In *O'Brien*, Barclays Bank was unable to enforce Mrs O'Brien's surety and could not obtain possession of the house.

The following recent cases illustrate the present position.

In *Massey v Midland Bank* (1995), W allowed her house to be used as security for her lover's overdraft but she had been deceived by her lover who had been told by the bank that he should tell W to take independent advice. The lover took her to see his own solicitors who explained the position to her while her lover remained in the room. She signed the charge and the solicitor informed the bank that she had been given independent advice.

The court held that the bank had been put on enquiry when they were approached but were entitled to think W had received the advice they had suggested, so they were not bound by the lover's fraudulent statements. They were not required to enquire as to all the details of W's meeting with the solicitor.

Note
W was not a cohabitee of her lover although she did have children by him and following *O'Brien* it was stated that a mortgagee will have notice of undue influence if there is joint ownership, so that if undue influence is established the mortgagee will not be allowed to enforce

his rights and that this applies to couples even if they do not cohabit in the property.

In *Banco Exterior Internacional v Mann* (1995), H also owned a business and borrowed money from the bank for it partly secured by a charge on the matrimonial home. The bank demanded that before they granted the charge H should make sure his wife knew that she should consult her own solicitor.

H gave the documents to his company's solicitor who informed the wife of them in a letter. Both H and W then went to this solicitor together and W signed the documents. H then defaulted and the bank sought possession of the matrimonial home.

The bank appealed against a judgment that there had been undue influence and the bank had had constructive notice of such because they had not ensured W had been adequately advised.

The appeal was allowed. The bank was entitled to rely on the company solicitor to give the necessary advice when the solicitor had certified that this was so.

In *TSB v Camfield* (1995), partners in business secured a loan from the bank by charges on their respective matrimonial homes, in which each of their wives had an interest. The bank asked its own solicitors to ensure that each wife received independent advice. The solicitors told the bank this had been done although the wives had only been seen when their husbands were present. One wife had only agreed because her husband had said the amount involved was only £15,000. In fact, the amount was unlimited although her husband had made an entirely innocent misrepresentation.

The Appeal Court held that since she had been innocently misled, she was not liable. She had not received independent advice and the bank had had constructive notice of her husband's inducement to obtain her surety.

In *Halifax Mortgage Services v Stepsky* (1995), H and his wife wanted money to pay off an existing mortgage and other debts, but they told the mortgagees that they wanted the loan to buy shares in the family business. The solicitor acting for them knew this. They then defaulted on the loan but the wife claimed that the mortgage should be set aside because she had been unduly influenced by her husband and that she should have been advised by the mortgagee to take independent advice.

It was held that the solicitor had a duty not to disclose the real reason for the loan unless H and W agreed, so that the mortgages could not be imputed to have known it and could not therefore have been aware of any undue influence. They had not been put on enquiry.

In *Credit Lyonnais Bank v Burch* (1996), an employee had guaranteed her employer's overdraft by a charge on her flat. She argued that she had been subject to undue influence even though the bank had advised her to take independent advice. The court held that she had been subject to undue influence and had suffered such a disadvantage that the guarantee to the bank would be set aside. The bank had not sufficiently advised her as to her transaction.

Implied consent to a mortgage

Where there is no undue influence, the mortgagees may be able to establish implied consent by the owner of a beneficial interest as in *Paddington Building Society v Mendlesohn* (1985) and other cases (see below).

Note

Where a mortgage is under the Consumer Credit Act (CCA) 1974, a court may look at extortionate credit agreements. This act has a limited role in mortgages because:

- it only deals with 'regulated consumer agreements', ie credit limited to £15,000 in the case of an individual or a partnership;
- it does not cover building society loans or loans from local authorities.

Section 138 of the CCA 1974 defines extortionate as 'grossly exorbitant' or payments which would otherwise grossly contravene the ordinary principles of fair dealing.

There are not many cases involving this Act, but note:

- In *Woodstead Finance Ltd v Petrou* (1986), an interest rate of 42% was not considered extortionate. The rate was not unusual in view of the risk involved.
- In *A Ketley Ltd v Scott* (1981), an interest rate of 48% *per annum* was not considered extortionate. The mortgagors had received advice; were of sufficient experience to know what they were doing; presented a high degree of risk; and, in addition, one of them had failed to inform the mortgagees he had already put a charge on the property.

The rights of the mortgagee

The mortgagee has the following rights.

The right to sue for breach of contract

A mortgage means that the mortgagor has made a covenant to pay back the money borrowed with any interest agreed. If he does not do this the mortgagee may sue him at common law, provided he does so within the 12 year period (s 20 of the Limitations Act 1980).

The right to possession of the mortgaged property

A mortgagee has a right to possession 'before the ink is dry' on the paper (*Four Maids Ltd v Dudley Marshall Properties Ltd* (1957)) unless there is a clause negating this in the mortgage deed. The mortgagor does not have to default for this to happen; it arises as soon as the mortgage is created.

In practice, possession is usually sought as a preliminary to sale. If this is not done, the mortgagee may find himself having to account for any money he has, or should have, received.

In *White v City of London Brewery Co* (1889) a brewery took possession and let the premises on condition that their beer was sold. They were made to account for the money they would have received had they let the premises as a free house.

Quennell v Maltby (1979) affirmed that possession requires a court order. A court has no right at common law to refuse such an order but may do so if it would be inequitable to grant it.

Where a mortgagee seeks possession of a *dwelling house*, the court has other powers under s 36 of the Administration of Justice Act (AJA) 1970 and s 8 of the AJA 1973 under which a court may:

- adjourn proceedings; or
- make an order but stay proceedings; or
- make an order but postpone possession,

providing there is a reasonable chance the mortgagor will be able to pay the arrears in a reasonable time. (The AJA 1973 no longer requires payment of the principal sum as well which is normally the case when there is default.)

In *Target Home Loans Ltd v Clothier* (1994), the Clothier mortgagor took a mortgage payable by instalments but fell into arrears. The mortgagees applied for a possession order but the judge exercised his discretion under s 36 of the AJA 1970, as amended by s 8 of the AJA 1973, on the grounds that the mortgagor would be able to pay the sums due in a reasonable time. This turned out not to be possible because the means of repayment of the arrears had collapsed, so the mortgagees appealed. This time the mortgagors stated they had put the property up for sale and had expected to sell quickly.

It was held that the court did have the power under s 36 to postpone possession even if the likelihood of payment of arrears in a reasonable time was because of the expected sale of the property. The mortgagors were given a three months postponement of the possession order.

National & Provincial Building Society v Lloyd (1996) affirmed that the court may suspend a possession order while a sale of the property by the mortgagor is being arranged, provided the sale will take place within a reasonable period and this is not merely a hope.

In this case, it was just a hope and suspension of the possession order was not granted.

Cheltenham and Gloucester Building Society v Morgan (1996) illustrates the power of the judge to delay possession. The case involved a house worth £225,000 held on a mortgage of £90,000. The arrears amounted to about £7,000. The judge held that the usual practice of construing a 'reasonable term' for payment of arrears as two years or more should not be regarded as the only one. Discretion under the amended s 36 of the AJA 1973 could be the remainder of the mortgage term.

Note
Where there are *commercial agreements* the court still has no power to grant possession, unless the whole mortgage payment can be made in reasonable time.

The right to sell the mortgaged property

This arises as soon as one instalment is due but unpaid (*Payne v Cardiff RDC* (1932)). This requirement is one of those in s 101 of the LPA 1925 which states that:

- the mortgage must have been made by deed; and
- the mortgage money must have become due; and
- there must be no contrary intention expressed in the deed.

Further, the power cannot be exercised until the requirements of s 103 of the LPA 1925 are satisfied. This occurs only when:
- the mortgagee has served notice on the mortgagor and the mortgagor is in default three months after this; or
- that there are at least interest arrears of two months; or
- the mortgagor is in breach of some covenant other than that to pay interest, or some other condition in the mortgage deed.

Note

In *Lloyd's Bank plc v Bryant* (1996), the court stressed that a mortgagee owes no duty to the mortgagor to exercise in a positive way any of his, the mortgagee's, rights and powers to sell and still less to refurbish the mortgaged property. Even if the receivers mismanage the property, there is no recourse from the mortgagees. The receivers are the agents of the mortgagor not the mortgagee. One of the complaints made was that the receivers had undervalued the property.

Should a mortgagee sell before the requirements of ss 101 and 103 are met, he may be sued for damages by the mortgagor.

The mortgagee is also required to adhere to certain conditions of sale
- *He must exercise his power to sell in good faith*
  This means he must take reasonable care to obtain the 'true market value'. In *Cuckmere Brick Co Ltd v Mutual Finance Ltd* (1971), property was sold with planning permission for houses but there was no indication that such permission had also been given for the building of flats. As a result, the purchaser obtained the land at a lower price than he would have had to pay if all the information had been available. The mortgagees were held liable for the difference in the price paid and the value which would have been put on the land had the permission been made known.

Note

The Building Society Act 1986 requires the 'best price reasonably obtainable'.

- *He must not sell to himself or his nominee*
  This means that he must ensure the sale is a *bona fide* one (*Williams v Wellingborough BC* (1975)).

But

the Privy Council in *Kwang Lam v Wong Chit Sen* (1983) indicated that there is no inflexible rule that a mortgagee may not sell to a company in which he or she has an interest. The circumstances of the case may mitigate the rule.

- *The mortgagee must act according to s 105 of the LPA 1925 and apply the proceeds of sale in the following order*
  (a) Payment of any encumbrances existing prior to the mortgage and which were not subject to the mortgage.
  (b) To pay the costs of the sale.
  (c) To discharge the mortgage and any interest due.
  (d) The balance to be paid to the mortgagor.

Note

In *Palk v Mortgage Service Funding* (1993), the mortgagors wanted to sell their house but were in a negative equity situation. The sale would mean no further mortgage interest would accrue. The mortgagee objected because the sale would still leave a debt. The mortgagee wanted instead, to let the house at a rent and sell when the housing market improved.

It was held that s 91 of the LPA 1925 gave the court a complete discretion to order a sale even if the mortgagees did not wish it.

In *Halifax Building Society v Thomas* (1995), a mortgagor defaulted and the mortgagee obtained a possession order and sold the property. The sale raised enough to pay the costs and the mortgage and there was a surplus. The mortgagee placed this in an account and then argued it was entitled to it on the grounds that it represented a profit on a fraudulently obtained mortgage so that it became theirs under a constructive trust. The court disagreed; the money was held for the mortgagor under s 105 of the LPA 1925.

The mortgagee's right to foreclose

This is virtually a right to confiscate the mortgagor's right to his property but it is rarely used and requires a court order which can only be obtained if:

- the legal date of redemption has passed; and
- a court action is undertaken.

The mortgagee's right to appoint a receiver

This power is given by s 109 of the LPA 1925 and is rarely used for dwelling houses.

Co-ownership and implied consent to a mortgage

Where a person claiming a beneficial interest in property which has been mortgaged has, by conduct, implied that he or she has consented to the mortgage, then the court will estop such person who is in occupation of the property from claiming such interest against a mortgagee or purchaser.

Midland Bank Ltd v Farmpride Hatcheries Ltd (1981). Where a person in occupation of mortgaged property refuses to state whether he or she has an interest in such property, or knowingly misleads an enquirer as to that interest, the court will estop such occupier from asserting that interest against a purchaser.

In *Paddington Building Society v Mendlesohn* (1985), a mother had a beneficial interest in property in which her son held the legal title. She knew her son was taking out a mortgage on this property. Her son defaulted on the mortgage payments and the Building Society sought possession.

The court held that the mortgagees could gain possession. The mother had implied her consent to the mortgage.

Equity and Law Home Loans v Prestidge Ltd (1992) is another case involving implied consent. The legal title to property was in M's name only. He mortgaged the property. The equitable co-owner knew of this mortgage. M then re-mortgaged the property and ran off with the money so raised, after settling the first mortgage.

It was held that the equitable co-owner was bound by the second mortgage. When she had impliedly consented to the first mortgage, she was bound by the second. This means the second mortgagee stepped into the place of the first mortgagee and so took priority over her beneficial interests.

The more recent case of *Castle Phillips Finance v Piddington* (1995) restricts the *Prestidge* case and re-emphasises *Camfield*. A husband persuaded his wife to use a house which she alone owned for security for his debts. She agreed that it be mortgaged to Lloyd's Bank. This was then replaced with a mortgage with Barclays Bank. She agreed to this second mortgage but did so because her husband had misrepresented the facts. H later replaced this Barclays mortgage by a third one with the plaintiffs by defrauding his wife.

The court held that the second mortgage with Barclays had been obtained, in part, by undue influence or misrepresentation and was, therefore, completely void. In this the court followed *Camfield*.

The third mortgagee, ie the plaintiff, could step into the shoes of the first (Lloyd's Bank) on the same terms, ie the same amount and conditions. In this the court restricted *Prestidge*.

The priority of mortgages

When there are concurrent mortgages there is the problem of which has priority. Where there is such a problem:

- Consider registered and unregistered land separately, and make a heading for each.
- Then, under each heading, arrange the mortgages in the order in which they were created.
- Then note the date of creation.

- Indicate which are legal and which are equitable.
- In another column indicate whether, and when, the mortgages were registered.

The protection of mortgage interests and priority

Unregistered land

Mortgages of unregistered land may be legal or equitable mortgages.

Legal mortgages

A legal mortgage protected by title deeds is good against the whole world and so always takes priority. A legal mortgage not protected by title deeds, ie a puisne mortgage, needs to be protected by registration as a Class C(i) land charge under the Land Charges Act (LCA) 1972. Remember that if there are title deeds the land will be unregistered land.

Equitable mortgages

Equitable mortgages are protected by deposit of title deeds. These come within the doctrine of notice; the purchaser will have notice because he would otherwise have had the title deeds.

An equitable mortgage of an equitable interest comes within the rule in *Dearle v Hall* (1823), ie the date of priority is the date on which the owner or the trustees of the legal estate were given notice in writing of the mortgage.

Note

The date is that of notice given not the date of creation.

Other equitable mortgages are registrable as Class C(iii) land charges under the LCA 1972. Remember for priority of equitable interests the equitable rule the 'first in time prevails' applies but for equitable interests in unregistered land this means that the first to be registered as a land charge (not the first to be created) takes priority. This is now given statutory force by s 97 of the LPA 1925.

Problems

A legal mortgage without title deeds is a puisne mortgage and is registrable as a Class C(i) land charge. An equitable mortgage may be registered as a Class C(iii) land charge. The rule that the first to be registered applies (s 97 of the LPA 1925) means that an equitable mortgage could take priority over a legal mortgage without title deeds, in other words, a puisne mortgage.

Where there are several puisne mortgages there appears to be a conflict between s 97 of the LPA 1925 and s 4(5) of the LCA 1972. Section 97(2) of the LPA 1925 requires priority be given to the first to be registered; s 4(5) of the LCA 1972 requires priority to be given to the first to be created if a later charge has not been registered. (In practice the problem does not arise.)

Example
John creates a puisne mortgage.
Mary creates a puisne mortgage.
John registers his mortgage.
Mary registers her mortgage.
Who has priority?
According to s 4(5) of the LCA 1972, Mary has priority because John had not registered his charge before hers was created.

According to s 97 of the LPA 1925, John has priority because his charge was created before Mary registered her charge.

Registered land

The two forms must be considered.

Legal mortgages
All legal mortgages should be registered. Priority is determined by date of registration.

Equitable mortgages
Priority is determined by the date of registration (not by date of creation). The Land Registration Act 1986 makes no distinction between equitable interests in registered and unregistered land; in both cases the date of registration prevails. If two equitable mortgages have both not been registered, then both are governed by the maxim 'where the equities are equal the first in time prevails'.

The Law Commission's Report on mortgages of land

The Law Commission considered mortgages of land, and in 1991 this resulted in a draft Bill in Parliament. The basis of the report is:

- that the law on mortgages needs simplifying;
- that there is one purpose, and one alone, for a mortgage and that is to provide security for a loan.

It proposed:

- A completely new system. All existing means of creating mortgages should be replaced. There should be an act creating two types of mortgage only: the 'formal land mortgage' and the 'informal land mortgage'.
- The 'formal land mortgage' would be required to be by deed. It could be for both legal and equitable interests and the mortgagee would have legal rights against a mortgagor who is in default. It would also allow the mortgagee to sell if an 'enforceable event' occurred, eg arrears or serious breach of covenant.
- The 'informal land mortgage' would also be available for both legal and equitable interests in land. It could be created by deed or in writing as required by s 2 of the LP(MP)A 1989. It would not give the same rights against a defaulting mortgagor so the mortgagee's rights would need to be protected in another way.
- There would no longer be a right to possession by the mortgagee but the court could grant possession if the property needed to be sold. The court would also be given wide powers to change the mortgage terms where it would be equitable to do so.

Question hints

Essay type questions

To answer these you must be thoroughly familiar with mortgages. Do not merely regurgitate material. Many questions will ask you to discuss an issue or quotation, or to comment on it, or give your opinion. Do not begin by stating what you think, indicate instead, what you think the question means (but do not repeat the question) and how you are going to tackle it. Deal with each point in turn and develop your essay logically. Each point will need to be considered from all points of view. If you have been clear and logical, by the time you reach your conclusion you should have an opinion to express! You will need to refer to cases but make sure they are apposite and you do not include irrelevant details.

Problem type questions

These may be confined strictly to mortgages but they may involve other issues, for example, co-ownership and beneficial interests.

You need to ask:

- Is this question about mortgages alone? Whom am I to advise, mortgagor or mortgagee? If it is the mortgagor does he want to get out of the mortgage or stop the mortgagee from getting possession? If so consider the mortgage agreement; was it straight forward or were there other agreements associated with it? Go through your list of the rights of the mortgagor and apply the facts of your problem to each right in turn using the relevant cases. Do *not* cite all the cases and all the facts in them. Look for facts which are analogous. If the mortgagee wants possession, has he done what he should to get it? Is it a dwelling house so that the AJA 1970 and AJA 1973 apply? If he wants to sell, have ss 101 and 103 of the LPA 1925 been complied with? If he has sold did he meet the requirements of s 105?

- Does this question involve more than one mortgage? If this is the case, ask yourself if it is registered or unregistered land, and whether the mortgages were legal or equitable, because priority of mortgages will be involved.

- Does the question involve anyone other than one legal owner? If it does, consider spouses or cohabitees who could have a beneficial interest (you may have to indicate how they have obtained it, eg resulting/constructive trust, but do not do so if the question states that the legal owner is holding for a spouse/cohabitee on a trust of land). Is there any implied consent to the mortgage by the beneficial owner? (*Paddington Building Society v Mendlesohn* (1985); see Chapter 3.)

Index